W9-DAZ-813

Lisbon

Berlitz Publishing Company, Inc.
Princeton   Mexico City   London   Eschborn   Singapore

Text:	Neil Schlecht
Editor:	Alice Fellows
Photography:	Neil Schlecht except pages 49, 70, 73, 80, 84, 88 by Claude Huber and pages 55 and 83 by Gignoux
Cover Photo:	Neil Schlecht
Photo Editor:	Naomi Zinn
Layout:	Media Content Marketing, Inc.
Cartography:	Ortelius Design

The author wishes to thank the Portuguese National Tourist Office in New York for its assistance making travel arrangements.

Although the publisher tries to insure the accuracy of all the information in this book, changes are inevitable and errors may result. The publisher cannot be responsible for any resulting loss, inconvenience, or injury. If you find an error in this guide, please let the editors know by writing to Berlitz Publishing Company, 400 Alexander Park, Princeton, NJ 08540-6306.

ISBN 2-8315-7697-0

Printed in Italy
010/102 REV

CONTENTS

● A (☞ in the text denotes a highly recommended sight

Lisbon

LISBON AND
THE LISBOÊTAS

In the history books, Lisbon's fortunes rise and fall dramatically over the course of its 3,000-year history, much as the city itself spills over innumerable hills along the Tagus River. Most likely founded by the Phoenicians, settled by the Romans, and the capital and port city of the world's greatest maritime power in the 15th and 16th centuries, Lisbon soon met with decline and disaster.

In 1755, the city suffered a massive earthquake, followed by encores of massive fires and tidal waves — an infernal episode straight from the pages of the Bible or a Hollywood script. Though some 40,000 residents perished and most of the old city was completely destroyed by the Great Earthquake, Lisbon found a way to rebuild. Though it wouldn't again reach its former heights, and in the 20th century would slip into a prolonged slumber, today Lisbon is again on the rebound.

In the recent past, though, Lisbon has been seen as a lovely but laid-back provincial capital, an outpost on the edge of Western Europe known more for the charms of the narrow Moorish-style streets, the beauty of its hand-painted ceramic tiles, and occasional ornate architectural flourishes than for economic dynamism. After decades of dictatorship, Portugal remained cut off from the rest of Europe, and Lisbon turned its back on the Tagus River and Atlantic Ocean, which had brought it to such prominence.

While the seafaring heritage and melancholy *fado* music that spills out of taverns are still very much a part of this city, Lisbon is fast becoming a modern cosmopolitan capital. Money and foreign investment have flowed in along with Portugal's 1986 induction into the European Union, and a full-scale building boom is on. Not since the rubble was cleared from the Great Earthquake has the contrast between old and new been greater.

Lisbon is an exceedingly pleasant city, one perhaps more notable for its understated beauty and easygoing friendliness than for world-class monuments, churches, or museums. Neighborhoods are charmingly clustered on the sides of hills — the city was said to have been founded, like Rome, on seven hills, but you'll quickly discover the number to be closer to two dozen — along the wide but placid Rio Tejo (Tagus River). There are gentle reminders everywhere of Lisbon's distant past: the Phoenician profile of the modern fishing boats; the Moorish expertise with painted tiles; the pained notes of fado's longing and lament.

The narrow whitewashed streets of the old Moorish neighborhood, Alfama, twist and turn; they remain the heart of a modest, working-class, inner-city village. Here and elsewhere, Lisboêtas decorate their balconies with flower pots, their walls with colorful tiles, and the sidewalks with mosaics. On a more utilitarian note, the faded and frequently crumbling façades of homes are festooned with lines of brightly colored laundry hung to dry.

Women dressed in black tote bags of bread and groceries up and down Lisbon's hills without complaint, but most visitors will opt for one of the charming antique electric trams that still make the run of the city. Wandering is almost always rewarded with the discovery of picturesque nooks, or brilliant panoramic views of the city's red-tiled rooftops tumbling out toward the river. Whether from one of the lookouts in Alfama, the gardens of St. George's Castle, or the top of Santa Justa, the turn-of-the-century iron elevator that lifts workers and residents from the *Baixa* (lower city) to the *Bairro Alto* (upper neighborhood), Lisboêtas are never at a loss for an opportunity to take in the whole of their city in its sun-kissed splendor.

The Vasco de Gama bridge holds the title of the longest bridge of its kind on the European continent.

In Lisbon, the Tagus nears the end of its winding journey from the mountains of eastern Spain, swelling into what is known as the Straw Sea — a poetic allusion to the golden reflections cast by the afternoon sun. The river passes through Lisbon and beneath two bridges that have each held the title of longest bridge of its kind in Europe: the Ponte 25 de Abril, after its inauguration in 1966, and the new Ponte Vasco da Gama, which opened in 1998. East of the city, the Tagus flows into the Atlantic Ocean, an opening that allowed daring explorers to set sail from Lisbon during Portugal's Golden Age and found the farthest-flung empire of the time.

Although the cold Atlantic lies only a few miles down river, Lisbon's climate and ambience feel decidedly Mediterranean. A sheltered, south-facing location and mild winters allow palm trees and bird-of-paradise flowers to flourish, and the balmy weather encourages an unhurried pace in this capital of nearly one million inhabitants. The capital of the modern and *European* Portugal is now choked with traffic, but there is always plenty of time to pause for a cup of coffee and gaze out at the river or up at the hills.

Lisbon's citizens have a quiet, modest dignity about them and are the most gracious of hosts. The streets teem with people of diverse ethnicity and dress. Many are recent immigrants from the African colonies of Portugal's imperial past — Mozambique, Goa, Cape Verde, Macau, or Angola — who arrived in Lisbon and soon founded their own little colonies, speaking a slightly softer Portuguese. Other major cities on the Iberian Peninsula, like Barcelona and Madrid, are rather homogenous by comparison. It's also remarkable, compared to other southern European cities, how many ordinary citizens are fluent in English.

The sadly erroneous image of Portugal as a poor rural cousin of Spain is quickly being washed away. Travelers arriving to experience it for the first time, or their first visit in a long time, will find a city and country still in tune with Portugal's glorious past, but invigorated by possibility in the new Europe.

Lisbon may be one of Europe's most ancient settlements, but the cataclysmic 1755 earthquake destroyed many of the city's finest churches and palaces. A prominent survivor is the Castelo de São Jorge (St. George's Castle), perched on top of Lisbon's highest hill. It was begun by the Visigoths, and expanded by the Moors, before being captured by Christian crusaders in 1147 after a four-month siege. The ramparts now protect quiet gardens with fabulous views.

The castle overlooks Lisbon's oldest and most picturesque neighborhood, Alfama. The working-class quarter, once home to the city's elite, survived the tremendous earthquake, but only the labyrinthine layout of the Moors remains. Belém, a residential suburb, is the city's most monumental district. It proclaims Portugal's Golden Age of Discovery, with the city's finest Manueline monuments.

The Baixa is lower, downtown Lisbon — a business district of Neo-Classical buildings, the stock exchange and government ministries, the city's principal thoroughfare, and grand squares. Most of the Baixa was lost to the natural disaster, but was quickly rebuilt on a grid.

The upper city, reached by trolley, elevator, or steep climb, is called the Bairro Alto. One of Lisbon's quintessential neighborhoods, it is home to much of the city's

The local trolley is the favorite mode of transport for Lisboêtas and visitors alike.

nightlife, including fado clubs, restaurants, and bars. Within the upper city is the chic district of Chiado. Though much of Chiado was razed by a devastating 1988 fire, it has been impeccably rebuilt and once again houses some of Lisbon's most elegant shops.

Lisbon's old charms and way of life haven't diminished, but the city has thrown itself into the new millennium with gusto. The theme of the moment, once again, seems to be renovation. As the city again embraces the river and the sea, old docks along the river have been transformed into some of the city's hottest restaurants and nightspots. Lisbon hosted the World Expo 98, and used the occasion to reinvigorate the run-down industrial eastern section of the city along the river (today the Parque das Nações, a high-tech architectural showcase). The Expo brought worldwide attention to Lisbon and Portugal, as did the Pope's visit to the famous pilgrimage site of Fatima in May 2000.

Like Madrid, Lisbon is surrounded by some of the country's most appealing towns, easy excursions by car or public transportation. To really experience Lisbon as its residents do, you'll need to get out of town. Within a half hour are the beautiful green countryside; the sparkling beach resorts Estoril and Cascais west of Lisbon; and legendary Sintra, one of the most charming towns in Europe, with palaces and aristocratic *quintas* (estates) lodged in the mountains with views of the coast. Even closer to Lisbon, the handsome Versailles-style palace at Queluz is a draw for visitors, including heads of state.

North of the capital are Óbidos, enclosed by a pristine medieval wall and fortress, too perfect to be true; two of the country's most impressive monasteries, Alcobaça and Batalha; and Fátima, which has drawn religious pilgrims since 1917. A relatively short trip to Lisbon — as little as a week — can take in a surprisingly large section of western-central Portugal.

But this part of the world is best discovered at an unhurried pace. One of the great joys is enjoying Portuguese cuisine and wine, whether at a simple country inn or at one of Lisbon's chic new spots swathed in modernist design. Local cooking owes much to the country's close ties to the sea: fresh fish, seafood, and soups hearty enough for a tired sailor's homecoming. One of the country's great secrets are its table wines, produced in virtually every region. They're affordable, unpretentious, and memorable — which, come to think of it, is not a bad description of Lisbon and its environs.

A BRIEF HISTORY

Though a legend surrounding Lisbon's birth claims
Ulysses as the city's founding father, most hardheaded
historians date the city's origins to around 1200 B.C., with
the establishment of a Phoenician trading station. Its name
was probably Alis Ubbo or Olissipo.

Primitive peoples had settled in the area thousands of
years before, attracted to its location on a calm river close to
the Atlantic Ocean. Around 700 B.C., Celtic tribes moved
into northern and central Portugal, and the coastal settlements were incorporated into the empire of Carthage.

Recorded history of the city begins in 205 B.C., when the
Romans ousted the Carthaginians and created the province
of Lusitania, though not without fierce resistance from the
Celts. Lisbon was proclaimed a municipality, and Julius
Caesar is said to have named it *Felicitas Julia* — something
akin to the "Joy of Julius."

The Romans built roads; cultivated grapes, wheat, and
olives; and bequeathed the Latin foundations of the
Portuguese language. However, Rome's grip on the Iberian
peninsula grew weak, and most of the region was overrun by
Vandals and other Barbarians from north of the Pyrenees.
Lisbon fell at the beginning of the fifth century A.D., after
which a succession of migratory tribes controlled the city
until the sixth-century arrival of the Visigoths, who provided
a welcome period of peace.

The Moorish Conquest

In 711 a great Muslim invasion fleet from North Africa crossed
the Strait of Gibraltar; in a matter of only a few years, the
Moors had conquered almost all of Iberia. Lisbon became a
thriving outpost under Muslim occupation. The neighborhood

of Alfama, the city's oldest and most charming residential area, retains its original Arabic name, along with twisting, narrow streets that creep up the hillside from the river.

Although Christians had maintained a precarious foothold in northern Portugal, it was not until 1139, when Dom Afonso Henríques declared himself the first king of Portugal, that their struggle to gain power met with some success. He defeated the Moors at the Battle of Ourique; Lisbon, however, eluded his grasp for another eight years — the Moors were too securely ensconced in what is now St. George's Castle.

In 1147 the king recruited a volunteer force from thousands of Flemish, Norman, German, and English crusaders on their way to the Holy Land. He convinced the crusaders to stay long enough to strike a blow against the Moors and — perhaps no less gratifying — to seize the booty of Lisbon. Joining forces, the Portuguese and the rogue crusaders besieged Lisbon for four months. As the Moors fled, the victors swept in to grab the loot left behind. A century later the reconquest of Portugal was finally complete;

Inês and Pedro

Inês de Castro and Pedro the Cruel are two tragic figures of Portuguese royalty who could have served as the models for Shakespeare's Romeo and Juliet. Pedro, heir to the throne, defied his family and lived for a decade with the Spanish beauty, one of his queen's ladies-in-waiting. In 1355, three noblemen slit the throat of Inês — a political assassination ordered by Prince Pedro's own father, Afonso IV. When he became king just two years later, Pedro exhumed her body, crowned it, and ordered all the nobles to kneel and kiss the skeleton's hand. Pedro and Inês are entombed together in the monastery at Alcobaça.

Afonso III (1248–1279) chose Lisbon as his capital.

The Golden Age

In a decisive battle, fought in 1385 at Aljubarrota (about 100 km/62 miles north of Lisbon), João of Avis, recently proclaimed João I of Portugal, secured independence from Spain. A new alliance with England was sealed in the 1386 Treaty of Windsor, outlining true and eternal friendship. A year later King João married Philippa of Lancaster, the daughter of John of Gaunt. Their third

These ramparts are remnants of the medieval past — Portugal's Golden Age.

surviving son Henry, Duke of Viseu, Master of the Order of Christ, would change the map of the world — he became known as "Henry the Navigator."

Prince Henry won his spurs at the age of 21 when he sailed from Lisbon with a daring expedition that captured the Moorish stronghold of Ceuta in 1415. It was his first and last act of bravado, for he then retired to the "end-of-the-world," the Sagres peninsula in the Algarve, where he established a school of navigation that gathered together astronomers, cartographers, and other scientists whose work multiplied the skills of mariners. Their expeditions redefined European understanding of the world. During Henry's lifetime, Portuguese caravels sailed far beyond the westernmost point of Africa. With the colonization of

Madeira and the Azores, the foundations of the future Portuguese empire were swiftly laid.

The king who ruled over Portugal's Golden Age of Exploration — and exploitation — was Manuel I, "The Fortunate," who reigned from 1495 to 1521. Discoveries made during this period assured his position as one of Europe's richest rulers: He could well afford to erect monuments as elegant as the Tower of Belém and as impressive as the Jerónimos Monastery. The architecture that eased Portugal from the Gothic into the Renaissance still bears his name: Manueline style is whimsically flamboyant and decorative, and rife with references to the sea.

The most significant expedition under Manuel's flag was Vasco da Gama's legendary sea voyage from Lisbon in the summer of 1497. Rounding what is now known as the Cape of Good Hope, Vasco da Gama found what Columbus had been

This ceramic-tile mural depicts Lisbon's riverfront square, destroyed in the 1755 earthquake.

looking for, but missed — the sea-route to the spices of the East. Reaching Calicut in India in 1498, Portugal put an end to the Venetian monopoly of the Eastern spice trade by assuming control of the Indian Ocean and attracting merchants from all over Europe to Lisbon. Further territories were discovered, although accidentally, in 1500, when the Portuguese explorer Pedro Álvares Cabral unwittingly reached Brazil.

Times of Trial

When Manuel died in 1521, he was succeeded by his son, João the Pious. With one eye on the ungodly ways of prosperous Lisbon and the other on the Inquisition in Spain, João invited the Jesuits to cross the border into Portugal and, in an effort to preserve both academic and moral standards, moved Lisbon's university to Coimbra, where it remains to this day (other universities have since been established in the capital).

Although the Inquisition in Portugal was never as powerful as it was in Spain, it relentlessly persecuted the "New Christians" — the Jews, who were all forced to embrace Christianity, including Spanish Jews who had been promised refuge in Portugal. Despite these witch hunts, an outbreak of plague, and such natural calamities as earthquakes, by the end of the 16th century Lisbon had attracted so many people from outlying areas that its population was estimated at 100,000.

Hard times followed, however. The population of the nation in general was sorely depleted, many having left for the new colonies. When the king (and cardinal) Dom Henrique died leaving no heir in 1580, Philip II of Spain marched in and forced the union of the two crowns. It took 60 years for the local forces to organize a successful uprising against the occupation. On 1 December 1640 — a date still celebrated as Portugal's Restoration Day — Spanish rule was finally overthrown, and the Duke of Bragança was crowned

João IV in a joyful ceremony in Lisbon's huge riverfront square, the Terreiro do Paço (today the Praça do Comércio).

His grandson, João V, enjoyed a long and glittering reign (1706–1750). As money poured in from gold discoveries in Brazil, the king spent it on lavish monuments and buildings. His best-known extravagance was the palace and monastery at Mafra, 40 km (25 miles) northwest of the capital. In another effort to enhance the grandeur of his court and country, the king convinced the pope to promote the see of Lisbon to a patriarchate.

Destruction and Rebuilding

The great divide between early history and modern times in Portugal falls around the middle of the 18th century. On All Saints' Day, 1 November 1755, as the crowds packed the churches to honor the dead, Lisbon was devastated by one of the worst earthquakes ever recorded. Churches crumbled, the waters of the Tagus heaved into a tidal wave, and fires spread throughout the city. The triple disaster is estimated to have killed anywhere between 15,000 and 60,000 people. Reminders of the nightmare are still found in many parts of Lisbon; the most dramatic is the shell of the Carmelite church on a hill above the city's main square, which has been open to the sky ever since the morning the roof fell in.

Routine problems of state were beyond the talents of the ineffectual José I (1750–1777), who could not be expected to cope with the challenge of post-quake recovery. So the task of rebuilding fell to the power behind the throne — a tough, ambitious, and tyrannical minister known as Sebastião José de Carvalho e Melo, who later became the Count of Oeiras but is best remembered as the Marquês de Pombal. Taking advantage of the power vacuum once the earth had stopped shaking, he mobilized all of Portugal's resources for the clean-up. Survivors were fed and housed, corpses disposed of, ruins cleared, and an ambitious project for a newly structured city laid out. Today the modern sections of the capital are aptly referred to as "Pombaline Lisbon."

Pombal's achievements are commemorated with his heroic statue, on top of a column at the north end of the Avenida da Liberdade in downtown Lisbon, a choked traffic circle usually referred to as "Pombal." A huge equestrian statue of José holds the main place of honor in the Praça do Comércio, where it was fawningly erected during his life-

Since the 1990s, Lisbon has been undergoing a great revival and restoration.

time. The king had a close brush with death in an assassination attempt in 1758, after which Pombal inaugurated a reign of terror, complete with public executions and widespread repression.

The Peninsular War

At the beginning of the 19th century, Napoleon managed to drag Portugal into the heat of Europe's conflicts. The situation became so perilous that the royal family fled to Brazil, courtesy of English boats at their disposal. Taking no chances, they remained there until 1821, ten years after the crisis was over.

When France pressured Portugal to abandon its traditional loyalty to England, Lisbon attempted to stay neutral. In 1807,

Napoleon demanded that Portugal do the impossible — declare war on Britain. Responding to the predictable veto, the French army under Junot marched in, setting up headquarters in the pink palace at Queluz, just outside of Lisbon.

Military miscalculations in the face of a British expedition sent Junot's army packing in 1808. Over the next few years, repeat engagements became notable victories for the combined Portuguese-British forces, who owed much to the strategic brilliance of the great British commander, Sir Arthur Wellesley (later the Duke of Wellington). After the textbook battle of the Lines of Torres Vedras, north of Lisbon, the French began a long retreat, sacking and looting as they passed. Napoleon's last outpost in Portugal was evacuated in the spring of 1811.

Civil War

Peace was still to prove elusive, and only 22 years later the country was again at war — this time pitting brother against brother. Pedro IV, previously emperor of Brazil (which had asserted its independence from Portugal), fought to wrest the crown from his absolutist brother, Miguel I. Pedro won, though he died of consumption only months later, at the age of 36. His adolescent daughter, Maria da Glória, assumed the throne. She married the German nobleman Ferdinand of Saxe-Coburg-Gotha, who built for her the astonishing Pena Palace above Sintra and fathered her five sons and six daughters. Maria II died in childbirth at the age of 34.

Premature and tragic deaths claimed many Portuguese royals, but in all the country's history only a single king was assassinated. On 1 February 1908, as the royal family was riding past Lisbon's vast Terreiro do Paço (now more commonly called the Praça do Comércio) in an open carriage, an assassin's bullet felled Carlos I. A few seconds later another conspirator fatally shot Carlos's son and heir, Prince Luís

Felipe. A third bullet hit the young prince Manuel in the arm. Thus wounded and haunted, Manuel II began a brief two-year reign as Portugal's last king. He was deposed on 5 October 1910 in a republican uprising supported by certain elements of the armed forces. The royal yacht spirited him to Gibraltar and later to England, where he lived in exile.

Modern Times

The republican form of government was as unstable as it was unfamiliar. Resignations, coups, and assassinations kept an unhappy merry-go-round of presidents and prime ministers whirling. The nation could ill afford a war; nonetheless, German threats to its African territories — among other motives — edged Portugal into World War I on the side of the Allies. On 24 February 1916, the Portuguese navy seized a group of German ships anchored in the Tagus, and the Kaiser replied with the inevitable declaration of war. A Portuguese expeditionary force sailed for the trenches of France.

The war's toll hastened the end of Portugal's unsuccessful attempt at democracy. After a revolution in 1926, General António Óscar Carmona assumed control, and two years later entrusted the economy to António de Oliveira Salazar, then an austere economics professor at Coimbra University. The exhausted Portuguese finances immediately perked up. In 1932 Salazar was named Prime Minister. His tough, authoritarian regime — the *Estado Novo* (New State) — favored economic progress and nationalism. He kept Portugal neutral in World War II, but permitted the Allies to use the Azores as a base.

When a massive stroke struck Salazar in 1968, the reins were handed over to a former rector of the University of Lisbon, Dr. Marcelo Caetano. In 1974, however, the armed

Lisbon's futuristic new train and subway station was designed by the Spanish architect Santiago Calatrava.

forces, discontented by hopeless colonial wars, overthrew the dictatorship in the so-called "Red Carnation" revolution. Portugal disengaged itself from Mozambique and Angola, its seething African possessions, and absorbed the million or so refugees who fled to a motherland most had never seen. The nation suffered several years of political confusion before adjusting to democracy.

   With its entry into the European Union in 1986, the pace of development suddenly quickened. Aided by the EU, Portugal became one of the fastest-growing countries in Europe. In 1998, Portugal hosted the World Expo in Lisbon, and in 1999, further consolidated its European membership by accepting the gradual introduction of the euro, the single currency also adopted by Spain, Italy, Germany, France, and others.

WHERE TO GO

As in many cities, it's best to organize your time and interests according to neighborhood. The Belém district holds several of the city's star visitor attractions, but other neighborhoods, like Alfama and the Bairro Alto, are better for dining, shopping, and lingering.

Lisbon's waterfront is an arc stretching nearly 32 km (20 miles) along the River Tagus (*Tejo* in Portuguese). At the western end is Belém and at the eastern extreme is the Parque das Nações, the site of Expo 98. A map shows that many of the top attractions in Lisbon are within walking distance of the river, but because of the hills and the way in which the sights are spread out, it isn't always very easy to go directly from one to the other.

You can travel cheaply and efficiently from place to place by public transport. Buses are quick and fairly straightforward. Antique trolley cars ply some routes, especially Alfama and the Baixa, and funiculars climb steep hills. Lisbon's Metro — the underground railway or subway — is modern and fast, but serves a limited area. Taxis are plentiful and fairly inexpensive. Parking is difficult or impossible on weekdays, so a car is best saved for out-of-town excursions.

Upon arrival, a guided city tour, whether by bus or ferry along the river, can be a good way to grasp the general layout (see page 112).

OLD LISBON

 Alfama

Alfama is Lisbon's most picturesque and fascinating area. Here, in a labyrinth of steep, crooked streets, alleys, and

---

The Panteão Nacional's cupola, seen from the River Tagus, was completed some 300 years after construction began.

stairways — a layout left by Moorish occupants of the city — little seems to have changed since the Middle Ages. The whole area is a jumble of tilting houses with peeling paint, pastel laundry hanging from windows, bars, and fish stalls. The streets are so narrow that it's not uncommon to overhear elderly women sharing gossip across balconies.

You are almost certain to get lost, but in this area — safe and easygoing by day — that's part of the attraction. Stick to the narrow streets; if you find yourself in a street wide enough for both a car and a pedestrian, then you have strayed from the Alfama area.

Either start at the southern extremity of the neighborhood — Largo do Chafariz de Dentro, where the new **Casa do Fado e Guitarra** (Fado and Guitar Museum) is located — or take the easier path, beginning at the top, at Largo do Salvador or Largo das Portas do Sol, and let gravity lead you back down towards the river.

For a stunning view of the district, pause at the **Miradouro de Santa Luzia** on a bluff on the edge of Alfama, just below Portas do Sol. The pretty balcony, covered with painted tiles and bougainvillea, looks over a

In Alfama, Trams 12 and 28 ramble along the streets up the hill to Alfama and back down past the cathedral to Baixa — your best bet for scaling this hilly neighborhood.

charming jumble of tiled roofs that cascade down to the river. In the quiet little park here, you're likely to find a mix of tourists and old men in black berets playing cards and shooting the breeze.

Look for the two remarkably detailed and dramatic *azulejos* (tile panels) on the wall facing the belvedere. One of them shows Lisbon's waterfront as it was before the Great Earthquake, while the other depicts with bloodthirsty detail the rout of the Moors from the Castelo de São Jorge (St. George's Castle) in 1147.

Just up the street is another terrific lookout point, with even more expansive views. A small café on **Largo das Portas do Sol** serves snacks and beverages; visitors have been known to remain here for hours on end.

Just above the Miradouro de Santa Luzia, an old palace has been filled with choice pieces of furniture, ceramics, silver, carpets, and tapestries from 16th- to 19th-century Portugal and its colonies, forming the **Museu de Artes Decorativas** (Decorative Arts Museum). Among the curiosities are children's rooms with mini-furniture and a primitive version of a fold-up sofa bed. The museum belongs to the Ricardo do Espírito Santo Silva Foundation, which was established in the 1950s by the banker of the same name.

Just beyond the dense quarters of the Alfama, but near enough to be linked to the neighborhood, are two of its top sights. Though you might have trouble navigating the crooked streets up to it, **São Vicente de Fora** (St. Vincent Beyond the Walls) is eventually impossible to miss. Its twin towers rise above a hillside east of the castle. Reconstructed in the 16th century around the time of the Inquisition, this Italianate building is huge by local standards, yet it succeeds in combining mass and grace. But the highlight is next door: On the right, as you face the altar, a heavy wooden door leads to the monastic cloister where the walls and courtyards are lined with azulejos, blue-and-white glazed tiles depicting scenes of 18th-century French life and leisure, along with the animal *Fables* of La Fontaine. A pantheon contains tombs of the Bragança kings and queens from the first of the dynasty, João IV, to the last, Manuel II. Even Catherine of Bragança, queen of Charles II of England, was buried here, having returned to Lisbon after his death.

Directly downhill, the grandiose marble church, with a high dome reminiscent of the Capitol building in Washington, is the **Panteão Nacional (Santa Engrácia)**. Construction began in the 17th century, but the cupola wasn't completed until 1966. Describing something as the "works of Santa Engrácia" is shorthand for calling it an endless task.

Santa Engrácia remained a church until a few years ago, when it was deconsecrated and became the national pan-

---

Azulejos, the hand-painted, glazed ceramic tiles omnipresent in Lisbon, are not merely decorative. After the Great Earthquake and fires devastated much of Lisbon and the surrounding area in the 18th century, they were widely used to protect buildings from going up again in flames. The name *azulejo* is thought to be derived from *al-zuleiq*, Arabic for small polished stone.

Beyond the Walls — dizzying view of the church and monastery of São Vicente de Fora.

theon, honoring the greatest men in Portuguese history with symbolic tombs in the sumptuous rotund. To one side are the real tombs of presidents of the republic. You can sometimes climb to the base of the dome for a view down onto the marble floor of the rotunda. The pantheon was being renovated in mid-2000, but should be open again by now.

Almost every hill in this part of town has a *miradouro* (belvedere), but the best panorama of all belongs to the **Castelo de São Jorge** (St. George's Castle), reached by the steep alley and steps that continue east from Rua de Santa Justa. From the ramparts, you look out across the Baixa to the Bairro Alto, down to the river and the Ponte 25 de Abril, as far as Belém.

The Moors who ruled Portugal between the 8th and 12th centuries tenaciously clung to their castle, but were finally dislodged

History looms large in the form of Sé Patriarcal, Lisbon's austere cathedral.

in 1147. The new proprietor, Dom Afonso Henriques, expanded the fortifications, but earthquakes as well as general wear and tear over the following centuries left little intact. Restoration has since given new life to the old ruins, even if that means that much of the castle is not original.

Aside from the sensational vistas and the chance to roam the battlements, the castle is worth a visit for the park gardens inside its walls. Platoons of birds strut around as if they own the place — not just transient pigeons and sparrows, but resident peacocks, pheasants, pelicans, flamingos, swans, geese, and ducks. A recent feature within the castle is the **Olisipónia** multimedia show, which depicts Lisbon from a historical perspective.

Many ancient cities are built round their cathedrals, set facing a square of civic buildings. Lisbon's **cathedral** (*Sé Patriarcal*) appears out of nowhere at a bend in the road (most easily reached from the center by continuing east on the extension of Rua da Conceição). Despite the lack of pomp and circumstance, this handsome cathedral has significant historic and artistic importance.

Begun as a fortress-church in the 12th century, its towers and walls suggest a beleaguered citadel. The church was damaged repeatedly by earthquakes during the 14th, 16th, and 18th centuries, so the architecture now ranges from Romanesque and Gothic to Baroque. In a chapel off the apse at the eastern end you can see a couple of sentimental 14th-century tombs. For more medieval memories, enter the 13th-century cloister.

Secrets of Alfama

Some of the Alfama area's lesser-known attractions are best stumbled across by accident, through an arch or around a blind corner.

Rua de São João da Praça. Here Portugal's first king, Dom Afonso Henriques, entered Lisbon through the Moorish wall on 25 October 1147.

Igreja de São Miguel (St. Michael's Church). Built in the 12th century and restored after the earthquake, it has a glorious ceiling of Brazilian jacaranda wood and a Rococo gilt altar screen.

Beco da Cardosa. This alley, with blind-alley offshoots, is the very essence of Alfama's appeal.

Igreja de Santo Estêvão (St. Stephen's Church). With a 13th-century octagonal floor plan, but rebuilt several times over the years, the overhanging back of the church nearly collides with the front gate of an old palace.

Beco do Carneiro (Sheep Alley). Ancient houses sag towards each other across a step-street barely wide enough for two people. Above, the eaves of the buildings actually touch.

Rua de São Pedro. Alfama's boisterous main shopping street and site of a fish market. Fishwives shriek amidst a cacophony of chickens, dogs, and children playing kickball.

Largo de São Rafael: The remains of a tower that was part of the Moorish defenses that were finally overwhelmed in 1147.

There, amid the signs of earthquake damage, you can see parts of pre-Roman and Roman statues, columns, and inscriptions. One old chapel has a brilliantly wrought iron screen complete with intricate Moorish and Romanesque designs.

A few steps down the hill, the little church of **Santo António da Sé,** built in 1812, honors Lisbon's revered native son and saint. Though he's known throughout the world as St. Anthony of Padua, to Lisboêtas he is Santo António de Lisboa. The crypt — which is all that survived the 1755 earthquake — was built on the spot where, according to local lore, St. Anthony's house stood. St. Anthony is the patron saint of women in the market for husbands; sometimes bridal bouquets are left at his altar in the cathedral, along with thanks for all of his good work. Pope John Paul II visited the church during his 1982 visit to Lisbon.

Toward the waterfront, at Campo das Cebolas, the **Casa dos Bicos** is worth a glance. The building, faced with sharp

pyramid-shaped stones, was built during the early 16th century and belonged to the illegitimate son of Afonso de Albuquerque, the Viceroy of Portuguese India.

The **Rua dos Bacalhoeiros** (Street of Cod-Sellers), on which the house stands, is lined with small shops. One sells corks for flasks and bottles of all

The pointy Casa dos Bicos stands among shops on the Rua dos Bacalhoeiros.

shapes and sizes, another is piled high with empty burlap sacks, while yet another stocks nothing but cans of Portuguese sardines and tuna — with or without openers. The west end of the street leads to the busy waterfront square, Praça do Comércio.

A Detour East: Two Museums

Just east along the riverfront are two worthwhile museums that don't easily fit into any major neighborhood. The **Museu Militar** (Military Museum), across the square from the Santa Apolónia station, is on the site of a foundry where cannons were cast in the 16th century. Among the exhibits is Vasco da Gama's two-handed sword, almost as tall as a man.

Much more interesting to most visitors is the **Museu Nacional do Azulejo** (National Azulejo Museum), devoted entirely to the art of the painted ceramic tiles that are on view everywhere in Portugal. The museum occupies much of the former Convento da Madre de Deus (1509), and includes a small double-decker cloister surrounded by tiles in Moorish-style geometric patterns. By official count, about 12,000 azulejos are on show here, from 15th-century polychrome designs to 20th-century Art Deco.

One treasure is the *Lisbon Panorama*, a 36 m- (118 ft-) long composition of blue-and-white painted tiles, recording every detail of Lisbon's riverside as it looked 25 years before the 1755 earthquake. Another is the fabulous interior of the small church of **Igreja da Madre de Deus,** a heady mix of

The first king of Portugal, Dom Afonso Henriques, ordered the remains of São Vicente, the patron saint of Lisbon, shipped from the Algarve to the capital. Two ravens faithfully escorted the saintly relics, which explains why many a Lisbon lamppost bears the symbol of a sailing ship with a bird fore and aft.

Rococo gilt and gorgeous azulejos. Side walls are adorned with blue-and-white tiles from Holland, two rows of enormous paintings hang above them, and the ceiling also serves as a giant canvas. Restoration of the main chapel should be completed by late 2000.

BAIXA (LOWER CITY)

 Praça do Comércio (Commerce Square) is one of few extravagant touches in understated Lisbon. Stately arcades and bold yellow government buildings line all three sides of the vast plaza; the fourth is open to the harbor, with Venetian-style marble stairs leading down to the edge of the water. Just east of the stairs is where Transtejo river cruises depart (see page 113).

The 1755 earthquake wiped out the entire complex of buildings around the plaza, then called the Terreiro do Paço (Palace Square) — the name by which it is still known to many Lisboêtas — after the Royal Palace, which had stood here for four centuries. The post-quake layout is more harmonious and stately, but remains part of many citizens' daily lives. They catch buses and trams here, while children climb iron sculptures.

Lisboa Card

Lisbon's tourism offices offer a discount "Lisboa Card" that entitles holders to free Metro (subway), bus, tram, and lift transportation; free entry into 26 museums and monuments; and discounts of between 10 and 50 percent in other places of interest, as well as discounts in some shops. The card (for one, two or three days; 2,100–4,500 esc.) covers nearly everything of interest to visitors, including sights outside Lisbon, such as the palaces in Sintra and Queluz.

The bronze statue of a man in a plumed helmet on horseback represents José I, patron of Lisbon's great city-planner, the Marquês de Pombal, who designed the square as the centerpiece of his rebuilding of Lisbon. Another sculptural flourish is the triumphal arch, depicting the Marquês and the explorer Vasco da Gama, connecting government buildings on the north of the square. The grand square has seen its share of watershed political events: King Carlos and his son were felled by assassin's bullets in the Praça do Comércio in 1908, and one of the first uprisings of the Carnation Revolution of 1974 was staged here.

The arch leads to **Rua Augusta**, the main thoroughfare of Pombal's 18th-century grid. The severity of the identically-sized

Climb aboard — Lisbon's Praça do Comércio offers sculptural flourishes both modern and historic.

The Elevador de Santa Justa, nearly a century old, now functions as a look-out point.

buildings is relieved by decorative touches, such as tiled façades with different designs and colors. Several of the houses have now been painted bright yellow, green, and blue. After the disaster of 1755, the buildings on these 15 side streets were constructed to be earthquake-proof. The business district is full of shops, banks, hotels, and small restaurants.

The fastest way to reach the Bairro Alto from here is by the **Elevador de Santa Justa** (built by Raúl Mesnier, and not by Gustave Eiffel as most reports claim), a 30 m- (100 ft-) high iron Neo-Gothic elevator inaugurated in 1902. Originally powered by steam, it was rebuilt in 1993. In May 2000, the upper passageway was blocked off, so the elevator, although still functioning, is being used exclusively as a look-out point. The upper platform affords sensational views of Lisbon's tiled rooftops and the São Jorge castle.

The north end of Rua Augusta runs into the **Rossio**, Lisbon's main square, once the scene of public hangings, bullfights, and burning of witches. Today, it is still the main center of activity in Lisbon — the place to window-shop, meet friends, watch the busy crowds go by from sidewalk cafés, and listen to the fountains and the cries of the newsboys and flower sellers. The Rossio (formally named Praça Dom Pedro IV) isn't as choked with diesel buses as it was just a few years ago, but it is still most popular place to catch a taxi or bus.

The statue on the column in the square honors the first emperor of Brazil, Pedro IV (1826–1834). On the north end of the square is the handsome **Teatro Nacional Dona Maria II**, and on the west side, one street removed, is the **Estação do Rossio** (railway station), which looks more like a Moorish palace with horseshoe arches. Actually, it's a romantic effort of the late 19th century in the style now formally known as Neo-Manueline. Like many buildings in Lisbon, it was still under renovation in mid-2000.

The Rossio backs right up to another major square, **Praça da Figueira.** This square is built around an equestrian statue of João I, founder of the Avis dynasty. It's usually draped with fluttering pigeons.

Just northeast is the **Praça Martim Moniz**, carefully renovated at the end of the 1990s and outfitted with fountains that function as a water park for kids, modern steel kiosks featuring handcrafts, and other small enterprises (including a tourism information kiosk and a couple of simple cafés). The views of Alfama and the castle district are lovely.

Back to the Rossio, a fairly straightforward obelisk marks the **Praça dos Restauradores,** which celebrates the overthrow of Spanish rule in 1640. Palácio Foz, the once-splendid palace situated on the west side of the square, now houses a **tourist information office**. Nearby, a funicular climbs to the top of the Bairro Alto (see page 37).

Tourists and office workers often recline on the massive, curved iron sculpture in the Praça do Comércio, catching a few zzz's or basking in the sun. It's perfectly all right to do so, but keep your camera and handbag wrapped around an arm or leg to prevent them from being stolen.

The Praça Martim Moniz has been recently outfitted with fountains that serve as a warm-weather waterpark for kids.

From here **Avenida da Liberdade** makes its way uphill for a little over 1 km (0.6 mile). The stately boulevard is graced with statues, fountains, ponds, flower gardens, cafés, and benches. The boulevard ends at the busy traffic circle called **Praça Marquês de Pombal** (or Rotunda), from which an elevated statue of the dictator (inexplicably accompanied by a lion) looks out over his rebuilt Lisbon.

BAIRRO ALTO (UPPER CITY)

Like the steep Alfama district, the Bairro Alto is a hilly and dense area full of picturesque old houses, their wrought-iron balconies hung with birdcages and flowerpots. The Bairro Alto is the nightlife epicenter of Lisbon. At night the sad songs of *fado* nightclubs spill out into the streets, as do bohemian revelers who bop from one disco or bar to another.

The easiest way to reach the Bairro Alto is to board the eccentric yellow funicular trolley at Praça dos Restauradores. Locals are just as apt to walk up the hill as wait for the funicular. At the top end of the brief journey is a lookout park, **Miradouro de São Pedro de Alcântara,** with an excellent view of the Castelo de São Jorge right across the Baixa.

Next to the *miradouro* lies the **Jardim Botânico** (Botanical Garden), reached through the university gate alongside the Academy of Sciences. It concentrates on the scientific cultivation of unusual plants from distant climes, but this serious activity doesn't disturb the lush, slightly unkempt beauty and tranquility. The tree-shaded gardens slope steeply downhill to a lower gate near the Avenida Metro station.

Two churches in the upper town are unusual enough to merit a visit. Just down the street from the top of the funicular, the **Igreja de São Roque**'s dull exterior (the original 16th-century facade perished in the 1755 earthquake) conceals several of the most lavishly decorated chapels in Lisbon. The Baroque altar of the chapel of São João Baptista (St John the Baptist), in front on the left, is a wealth of gold, silver, bronze, agate, amethyst, lapis lazuli, ivory, and Carrara marble. In 1742, João V of Portugal sent orders for this altar to Rome, where teams of artists and artisans worked on

A sprawling mosaic is among many treats found along Avenida da Liberdade.

Lisbon Highlights

Museums are generally open Tues–Sun 10am–5pm (some stay open until 6pm or 6:30pm in summer). Many close for lunch between 12:30 or 1pm and 2 or 2:30pm. Entrance charges usually range from 400 esc–600 esc, but in many cases are waived on Sunday morning or throughout the whole day.

Castelo de São Jorge (St. George's Castle). Tram 28; bus 37 from Praça da Figueira. The old citadel of the Moors commands impressive views of the city from its ramparts. The castle has been restored and has pleasant gardens within its walls. Open daily 9am–9pm. Olisipónia multimedia show, daily 10am–7pm. Free. (See page 27.)

Sé Patriarcal (Cathedral). Largo da Sé; Tel. 21-88 67 52. Tram 28, or a short walk from Praça do Comércio. A fortress-like church begun in the 12th century and featuring fine tombs. Open Mon–Sat 10am–5pm. Open daily 10am–5pm. Free; entrance to the cloisters and museum of treasures, 100 esc. (See page 28.)

Alfama district. Tram 28; bus 37 (walk down). The oldest section of Lisbon: a distinctly Moorish labyrinth of stone stairs and alleyways, white-washed houses, and red-tiled roofs. Igreja de Santo Estêvão is a fine 13th-century church in the midst of this modest neighborhood. Free. (See page 23.)

Mosteiro dos Jerónimos. Praça do Império, Belém; Tel. 21-362 00 34. Tram 15 from Praça do Comércio; bus 43 from Praça da Figueira. Belém's massive monastery, dating from the early 16th century, has impressive Manueline cloisters and architectural embellishments. Open Tues–Sun 10am–5pm. Church free; Manueline cloisters, 500 esc. (See page 44.)

Torre de Belém. Avenida de Brasilia, Belém; Tel. 21-362 00 34. Tram 15 from Praça do Comércio; bus 43 from Praça da Figueira. This famous decorative 16th-century tower is regarded as the epitome of Portugal's Manueline architecture. Open Tues–Sat 10am–5pm; 500 esc. (See page 47.)

Museu Nacional de Arte Antiga (Museum of Ancient Art). Rua das Janelas Verdes; Tel. 21-396 41 51. Tram 15 or 18; bus 7, 49, or 27 from Rotunda (Praça Marquês de Pombal) or Belém. Portugal's largest museum, an excellent collection of old masters, silver, gold, ceramics, and Oriental treasures, including

Nuno Gonçalves's *Adoration of St. Vincent* and Hieronymus Bosch's *The Temptations of St. Anthony*. Open Wed–Sun 10am–6pm; Tues 2pm–6pm. 500 esc. (See page 41.)

Museu Calouste Gulbenkian. Avenida de Berna, 45 at Praça de Espanha; Tel. 21-793 51 31. Metro: São Sebastião or Praça de Espanha; bus 31, 41, 46 from Rossio and Rotunda. A superb collection, constructed by an Armenian oil billionaire resident in Portugal, of ancient art, ceramics, textiles, sculpture, and paintings. Open Wed–Sun 10am–6pm, Tues 2pm–6pm. 600 esc. (See page 49.)

Museu Nacional do Azulejo/Convento da Madre de Deus. Rua da Madre de Deus, 4; Tel. 21-814 77 47. Bus 18, 42, or 105. A collection of gorgeous 16th- to 18th-century painted ceramic tiles, occupying an old convent with a spectacular church. Open Wed–Sun 10am–6pm; Tues 2pm–6pm. 600 esc. (See page 31.)

Museu dos Coches. Praça Afonso de Albuquerque, Belém; Tel. 21-895 59 94. Tram 15 or 17 from Praça do Comércio; bus 27 from Rotunda. Lisbon's most popular museum, a collection of 16th- to 19th-century royal and other coaches and carriages. Open Tues–Sun 10am–5:30pm. 600 esc. (See page 43.)

Mosteiro de São Vicente de Fora. Largo de São Vicente; Tel. 21-887 64 70. Tram 28; bus 12. A 16th-century monastery and church with fabulous azulejos lining the cloisters, one series inspired by La Fontaine's *Fables*. Excellent views from terrace. Open daily 9am–12:30pm and 3pm–6pm 500 esc. (See page 26.)

Museu-Escola de Artes Decorativas (Fundação Ricardo Espírito Santo Silva). Largo das Portas do Sol; Tel. 21-886 19 91. Tram 12, 28; bus 37. A handsome collection of furniture, textiles, silverware, porcelain, and paintings from the 15th–19th centuries, on display in a Portuguese manor house. Open daily 10am–5pm. 800 esc. (See page 25.)

Oceanário de Lisboa. Parque das Nações; Tel. 21-891 70 02. Metro: Oriente. Europe's largest aquarium, designed for Expo 98, with five main habitats, including a central seawater tank the size of four Olympic swimming pools. Open daily, 10am–7pm. 1,700 esc; children, 900 esc. (See page 53.)

it for five whole years. After the pope had given his blessing, the incredible prefabricated masterpiece was dismantled and shipped to the customer. In an annex to the church, the **Museu de Arte Sacra** (Museum of Sacred Art) contains a collection of precious reliquaries, delicately worked jewelry, and vestments.

On Largo do Carmo, at the eastern edge of the Bairro Alto, the **Igreja do Carmo** (Carmelite Church) is rich only in memories. Today it stands in ruins, a mere shell, but an evocative reminder of the 1755 earthquake's tremendous destruction — the roof fell in on a full congregation on All Saints Day. The foundations date to the 14th century.

A very modest archeological museum is housed inside the only part of the church that has a roof over it; it is a hodgepodge of prehistoric pottery, Roman sculptures, a few

The Chiado district has been reborn since the devastating fires that ravaged the area in 1988.

early Portuguese tombs, and even a few ancient mummies under glass.

The longer and slower way downhill weaves through the very chic **Chiado** district, whose zigzagging streets have long been renowned for dispensing Lisbon's most elegant goods — silverware, leather, fashions, and books — along with fine pastry and tea shops. In 1988 the area was devastated by fires that wiped out two of Europe's oldest department stores, including the legendary Armazéns do Chiado. Portugal's most famous architect, the modernist Álvaro Siza, oversaw the tastefully reserved reconstruction of the neighborhood, especially the apartment houses and stores along Rua do Carmo and Rua Garrett.

The **Museu do Chiado**, on Rua Serpa Pinto, is a repository of late-19th and early 20th-century art, most of it Portuguese. The building, a former factory, was renovated in high style by the French architect Jean-Michel Wilmotte.

LAPA

Moving west and down toward the river from Chiado is the elegant residential neighborhood called Lapa. It is home to foreign embassies, tony homes, and several intimate hotels, but to most visitors it is known as the address of the **Museu Nacional de Arte Antiga** (National Museum of Ancient Art), Portugal's largest museum. It's housed in a large and handsomely designed palace on Rua das Janelas Verdes. The three-level museum is an absorbing place with at least three masterpieces of international renown, one on each floor.

On the top level, *The Adoration of St. Vincent,* a multi-panel work taken from Lisbon's São Vicente de Fora convent (see page 26) is attributed to the 15th-century Portuguese master, Nuno Gonçalves. It is a spectacular portrait of contemporary dignitaries, including Henry the Navigator.

Dozens of others are shown in every range of *distractio* — ire, boredom, and amusement — while several of the assembled clergymen appear as ugly, evil, or both.

Tram 15 makes the waterfront trip to Belém from Praça do Comércio; bus 43 from Cais do Sodré (just west of Praça do Comércio) covers virtually the same route.

On the second floor is an outstanding collection of 16th-century Japanese folding screens, in a small room all by themselves. The arrival of the Portuguese in Japan, seen through the eyes of the Japanese, is the theme of these extraordinary historical documents. Almost all the foreigners are portrayed as villains, while the locals, watching from their balconies, appear to be amused.

On the first floor a triptych by Hieronymus Bosch, the Flemish artist who painted surreal allegorical scenes with alien creatures, is both entertaining and horrific. *The Temptation of St. Anthony*, painted around 1500, is a fantastic Bosch hallucination, tempered with humor and executed with mad genius. A crane rigged up like a helicopter, flying fish taxis, and horse-size rats fill this ghoulish nightmare.

There's also an extensive collection of English, Flemish, Dutch, German, French, Italian, and Spanish painting of the 14th–19th centuries; china, and glassware from Europe and the East; rare Portuguese furniture and tapestries; and a room of ancient sculpture.

West of the Bairro Alto lies a delightful park called **Jardim da Estrela**, after the distinguished 18th-century church across the street. The 19th-century park contains abundant tropical foliage, plus the customary ducks, geese, peacocks, and pheasants, as well as a belvedere offering yet another angle on the city and its harbor. Just beyond the park is the **English Cemetery**, where the British writer Henry Fielding is buried.

BELÉM

Belém (Portuguese for Bethlehem), Lisbon's primary monumental district, is a suburb about 6 km (4 miles) west of Praça do Comércio. Land reclaimed from the river has been fashioned into parkland and marinas. Though the shore is unrecognizable today, the great Portuguese voyages of discovery in the 15th and 16th centuries set out from here.

Start a visit to Belém at the edge closest to central Lisbon. The **Museu Nacional dos Coches** (National Coach Museum) is housed appropriately in the former riding school of the Belém Royal Palace. Two grand halls display dozens of impressive carriages, drawn by royal horses for ceremonial occasions in both the city and cross-country over four centuries. The most extravagant are three sculpted, gilt car-

The 16th-century Mosteiro dos Jerónimos is considered a testament to a confident and faithful nation.

riages used by the Portuguese embassy in Rome in the early 18th century to impress Pope Clement XI.

Only a short stroll westward along the Rua de Belém is Lisbon's largest and most impressive religious monument, the **Mosteiro dos Jerónimos** (Jerónimos Monastery). Commissioned by Manuel I with the windfall of riches brought back by Portuguese ships from the East, the monastery is an obvious testament to a confident and faithful nation. The convent wing was destroyed in the 1755 earthquake, but the church and cloister survive, testaments to 16th-century style.

The vast south façade of the church, parallel to the river, is mostly unadorned limestone, making the few embellishments all the more remarkable. The main portal is a brilliant example of intricately carved stonework, as are the church's tall Manueline columns (which bridged the gap between Gothic and Renaissance styles in Portugal; see page 16). The effect is one of immense height and space. The first architect in charge was a Frenchman called Diogo Boytac, who was succeeded by the Spaniard João de Castilho, responsible for the cloister and main portal.

Inside the church are the royal tombs of Manuel I, his wife Dona Maria, and others, set on pompous sculptured elephants, a tribute to the newly discovered marvels of the East. Near the west door are the modern tombs of two giants of Portugal's Golden Age, Vasco da Gama and the poet Luís de Camões.

Once you leave the church (don't miss the fine sculptural work surrounding the exterior of the west portal), turn right for the cloister, an airy two-level structure of strikingly original proportions and perspectives. Note the clever intersection of both sharp angles and arches. No two columns are the same.

Across from the Mosteiro dos Jerónimos, the Centro Cultural de Belém offers a modern architectural juxtaposition.

The west section of the monastery has been largely restored and now houses the **Museu Nacional de Arqueologia** (the National Museum of Archeology), an important collection of ancient relics, including Bronze Age jewels, Stone Age tools, and from Roman days, excellent sculptures as well as mosaics.

The educational attractions continue just to the west with a **Planetário** (Planetarium), financed by Portugal's ubiquitous benefactor, Calouste Gulbenkian.

In the west end of the monastery and overflowing into new buildings beyond, the **Museu da Marinha** (Naval Museum) will appeal to anyone interested in history or the sea. Vast model ships of all the ages, often obsessively intricate, are displayed. Perhaps one of the most startling exhibits is the

The Padrão dos Descobrimentos — a monument to Portugal's seafaring expeditions and once-expansive empire.

huge galliot, or brigantine, built in 1785 to celebrate a royal marriage, with seats for 80 oarsmen. Next to it is the sea-plane which first flew the South Atlantic.

Across the road is the **Centro Cultural de Belém**, a modern building constructed in 1992. It houses a design museum and itinerant art exhibitions, and holds concerts in its auditoriums.

The modern **Padrão dos Descobrimentos** (Monument to the Discoveries), built in 1960 to commemorate the 500th anniversary of Henry the Navigator's death, juts from the riverbank like a caravel cresting a wave. On the prow stands Prince Henry, looking out across the river and wearing, as always, his funny round hat. The figures behind him represent noted explorers, astronomers, mapmakers, chroniclers, and others instrumental in Portugal's Age of Discovery. An elevator followed by stairs leads to the top and a superb view.

An interesting museum on the waterfront, the **Museu de Arte Popular** (Popular Art Museum) surveys the folk art and customs of Portugal, region by region, with plenty of charming fabrics, embroidery, furniture, toys, and dolls.

Finally, there is the famous **Torre de Belém** (Tower of Belém), erected in 1515 to defend the entry to Lisbon, and one of the finest examples of Manueline architecture. After crossing the wooden bridge, climb several floors to a top-level terrace that looks out over the Tejo. Though the often-photographed monument may be smaller than you imagined,

Manueline Architecture

The Portuguese may be principally known for *azulejo* designs and port wine, but equally important is the ornate style of architecture and stone carving that suddenly appeared in Portugal in the late 15th century. It flourished for only a few decades, for the most part coinciding with the reign of Manuel I (1495–1521), for which it was christened "Manueline."

Probably triggered by the great ocean voyages of discovery, it took late Gothic as a base and added fanciful decoration, dramatic touches that were frequent references to the sea. Stone was carved like knotted rope and sculpted into imitation coral, seahorses, nets, and waves as well as non-nautical designs. The style first appeared in the small Igreja de Jesus in Setúbal, Lisbon's Torre de Belém, and the Mosteiro dos Jerónimos. The style reached a peak of complexity in the unfinished chapels of the monastery at Batalha (see page 74). In the early 16th century, the style fell out of favor, and by 1540 Portugal had joined with the rest of Europe in building in the more sober Renaissance style.

it must have been a wonderful sight to weary explorers returning from their journeys.

While you're at this end of town, don't miss the **Palácio da Ajuda**, the biggest palace inside the city limits, which brims with all kinds of art works and curiosities. Portugal's Luís I (1861–1889), along with his Italian bride, Princess Maria Pia of Savoy, became the first royal to live here, outfitting the palace with lavish furnishings: Gobelin tapestries, Oriental ceramics, and rare Portuguese furniture. The palace is north of Belém up Calçada da Ajuda.

Mr. Five Percent

At the dawn of the Oil Age, a far-sighted Turkish-born Armenian put up money to help finance drilling in Mesopotamia (now Iraq), then part of the Turkish empire. For his part, he received five percent of the Iraq Petroleum Company.

Two world wars and the fueling of millions of cars, planes, and ships made Calouste Gulbenkian rich beyond imagination. He became a knowledgeable and dedicated collector of antiquities and great art, beginning with Turkish and Persian carpets, Armenian and Arabic manuscripts, and Greek and Roman coins. His passions spread to include ancient Egyptian art, Chinese porcelain, and Western painting. His mission was acquiring perfect examples in each of his chosen fields.

Gulbenkian was preparing to travel to the United States when he fell ill in Lisbon. He was so impressed with his treatment here that he decided to stay, and he established a philanthropic foundation to which he left most of his money and his collections when he died in 1955. The Gulbenkian Museum is his centerpiece, complemented by several other cultural facilities in Portugal, including the Modern Art Center, regional museums, a planetarium, and educational institutes.

NORTH LISBON

At the north end of Avenida da Liberdade, beyond the Marquês de Pombal rotunda, is a formal park, **Parque Eduardo VII**. The well-manicured lawns and shrubs are surrounded on either side by wooded areas and gardens. So thrilled were the Portuguese by a royal visit at the turn of the century that they named the park after England's king, Edward VII.

Lisbon's most original botanical triumph occupies the northwest corner of the park. Known as **Estufa Fria** (the Cold Greenhouse), this tropical rainforest right in the heart of a European capital contains plants and flowers from Africa, Asia, and South America.

North of Parque Eduardo VII, off Avenida António Augusto Auiar, is Lisbon's most remarkable museum, **Museu Gulbenkian** (Gulbenkian Museum). It was created to house one of the finest private collections in Europe, acquired by

an Armenian billionaire, Calouste Gulbenkian, and later bequeathed to Portugal. A great philanthropist who died in Lisbon in 1955, Gulbenkian meticulously acquired acclaimed masterpieces to mount his ideal and wide-ranging collection.

Surrounded by its own perfectly planned and maintained park, the huge collec-

The Estufa Fria, located in Parque Eduardo VII, is a botanical tour de force.

Formerly a source of fresh water for the Lisboêtas, the Aqueduto das Águas Livres is a major city landmark.

tion begins chronologically, with Egyptian ceramics and sculptures dating back to around 2700 B.C., delicate and perfectly preserved. The handsome statue of the Judge Bes is inscribed with hieroglyphs that date it from the reign of Pharaoh Psamtik I (7th century B.C.).

A large section of the museum is devoted to art of the Islamic East, and includes ancient fabrics, costumes, and carpets, plus ceramics, glassware, and illuminated pages from the Koran. The survey of Western art begins in the 11th century with illuminated parchment manuscripts. Tiny ivory sculptures of religious scenes come from 14th-century France, and there are some well-preserved tapestries from the Flemish and Italian workshops of the 16th century.

Paintings by Dutch and Flemish masters include works by Hals, Van Dyck, and Ruysdael. Pride of place is given to two Rembrandts: the sensitive portrait *Figure of an Old Man* and a painting of a helmeted warrior believed to be Pallas Athene or Alexander the Great (probably modeled by Rembrandt's son Titus).

The impressive hall of Chinese porcelain starts with the Yuan dynasty (13th–14th century; around the time of Marco Polo) and goes on to some exquisite 17th- and 18th-century items. Miraculously unmarred by the forces of time, each piece is representative of the pinnacle of a particular school of art.

The last room of the museum contains 169 items by Gulbenkian's friend René Lalique (1860–1945), the talented and versatile French jeweler. On display are Art Nouveau pendants, bracelets, necklaces, brooches, and combs of assorted materials and unexpected motifs.

The museum reopened in May 2000 after a lengthy renovation. Also part of the Calouste Gulbenkian Foundation are exhibition halls; concert halls, where musical performances and ballets take place (see page 84); and a center of modern art; as well as a library, a bookstore, and a restaurant.

A landmark most often seen by those heading out of town is the soaring arches of **Aqueduto das Águas Livres** (a fresh water aqueduct), which spans 18 km (11 miles) across the Alcântara valley north of downtown Lisbon. Fresh water was first carried across the aqueduct in 1748.

Along with the motorway to Cascais (see page 64), the aqueduct slices through the city's biggest park, **Monsanto**. Eucalyptus, cypress, cedar, umbrella pines, and oak trees all thrive on the rolling hillsides. Aside from calm and fresh air, the park contains sports grounds, bars, and restaurants. Its municipal campground ranks as one of Europe's prettiest and best organized, and the park also has some impressive *miradouros* (lookout points), giving outstanding views over

Lisbon and the estuary. Be warned, though, its roads usually turn into a huge traffic jam at rush hours.

Parque das Nações (Expo 98)

Lisbon, and the whole of Portugal, pinned much hope on the hosting of the World Expo in 1998. Celebrating the "Heritage of the Oceans," it was an opportunity for the nation to pay tribute to its former maritime greatness and reintroduce itself to the world. At least in the short term, the plan seems to have worked, since visitors to Lisbon and the rest of the country, intrigued by what they heard about Expo 98, are way up.

Unique structures remain from the World Exposition, held in Lisbon in 1998.

Lisbon used the occasion to reinvigorate a dirty industrial area east of the city, creating a high-tech entertainment park, along with new shopping and nightlife areas. A futuristic railway station (Gare Intermodal de Lisboa, by the Spanish architect Santiago Calatrava), a pristine shopping mall, and the stark white Vasco da Gama bridge extending across the Tejo — now Europe's longest bridge at 7 km (4 miles) — frame the park. Now that the Expo has come and gone, the **Parque das Nações** (Nations Park) complex, which extends 5 km (3 miles) along the riverfront, principally draws visitors to its world-class aquarium, which served as the

Oceans Pavilion during the Expo and has since become one of the city's primary attractions. The complex won the award for best urban development in Iberia in 1999.

Designed by the American Peter Chermayeff, the **Oceanário de Lisboa**, which looks something like a marooned oil derrick or space station from the set of a sci-fi thriller, is one of the largest and finest aquariums in the world, outclassing those in Sydney and Barcelona. It has five large tanks representing different oceans (Antarctic, Indian, Pacific, and Atlantic) with more than 10,000 samples of marine life and 200 species taken from the deep blue oceans. As visitors make their way around the massive circular aquarium — the size of four Olympic-size swimming pools — tiger sharks, manta rays, and schools of brightly colored fish glide silently by, overhead and underneath observation decks.

Nations Park is a good place for families, even though it can be devoid of life during the week. There are whimsical fountains,

An array of sea creatures from around the globe can be observed at the world-class Oceanário de Lisboa.

paddle boats, garden playgrounds, bowling lanes, aerial cable cars, and a tower with an observation deck — the tallest structure in Portugal — that looks out to the Atlantic and back down the river at Lisbon. Two former pavilions, Macau and the Knowledge Pavilion, remain open.

Sporting events, such as basketball and tennis, and concerts by performers like Pearl Jam and Caetano Veloso are held at the mushroom-like **Atlântico Hall** arena, which functioned as the Utopia Pavilion during the Expo. Many restaurants and bars are actively moving into the marina area, transforming it into an animated nightspot, and hotels and residential housing are being built, creating a newly desirable suburb east of Lisbon.

Among the former pavilions notable for their architectural interest, the **Portugal Pavilion**, by the Pritzker-prize winning Portuguese architect Álvaro Siza Vieira, is a standout. Siza's minimalist designs have won him worldwide acclaim. The pavilion features an astoundingly curved and suspended roof 67 m (221 ft) long and weighing 1,400 tons. Rain cascades off it like a perfectly controlled waterfall.

ACROSS THE RIVER TAGUS

The **Ponte 25 de Abril**, across the River Tagus, became the longest suspension bridge in Europe when it was opened to traffic in 1966. Originally named in honor of the nation's long-time dictator, after the Revolution of 1974 the name "Salazar" was removed, and for quite a time it was known simply as "the bridge." In an about-face, it was renamed for the revolutionary date, 25 April.

Just across the river, above Cacilhas and looming up over the bridge's tollbooths, is Lisbon's take on Rio de Janeiro's landmark, the statue of **Christ the King**. Almost 30 m (99 ft) tall, it stands on a modern four-pronged pedestal, with a church, the Santuário de Cristo Rei, housed in the base of the

Named for the Revolution of 1974, the Ponte 25 de Abril is a focal point of nocturnal Lisbon.

monument. Take the lift up to the viewing terrace for a glorious 360-degree **panorama** of the estuary, the bridge, all of Lisbon, and a vast expanse of Portugal to the south. To visit the statue you can drive across the bridge or take one of the **ferryboats** from Praça do Comércio to Cacilhas and then a taxi or a bus marked CRISTO REI.

EXCURSIONS FROM LISBON

One of the great attractions of Lisbon is the number of desirable excursions only a very short distance from the capital — there are highlights west, south, and north of the city. Whether you're looking for grand palaces, beach resorts, a perfectly preserved village enclosed by medieval walls, awe-inspiring abbeys, a charming romantic town lodged in the mountains, or a world-famous religious shrine, there's plenty to explore in the environs.

☛ Queluz

An easy half-day outing is to Queluz, 14 km (9 miles) west of Lisbon, home to the pretty pink palace commissioned by Pedro III (see page 67).

The sumptuous summer **palace** was built in the second half of the 18th century by the Frenchman Jean-Baptiste Robillon and the Portuguese Mateus Vicente de Oliveira. As a working official residence for the royal family, Queluz thrived mostly during the reign of Maria I (1777–1799). The queen is best remembered for her madness and shrieking fits at the palace.

From the road, the palace seems relatively unprepossessing, but inside, Portuguese modesty is totally abandoned, and

Lions and wolves once roamed through the labyrinthian gardens of the Palácio de Queluz.

Queluz is a model of only slightly tattered splendor. Though the palace lost much to French invasions (it was used by Junot as his headquarters during the Peninsular War) and a 1934 fire, it manages to preserve an air of 18th-century royal privilege. The **throne room** is one of the most lavish, with overpowering chandeliers and walls and ceilings layered with gilt. The **Sala dos Embaixadores** (Hall of Ambassadors) has a floor like a huge chessboard in addition to a wealth of mirrors and a *trompe l'oeil* ceiling. Queluz is rather curiously laid out — public rooms almost incoherently border living quarters.

> Most museums in Portugal are closed on Monday, but Queluz takes Tuesday off — and any other day when visiting heads of state are in residence.

The **Palace Gardens** are the pride of Queluz and are never-ending, with clipped hedges in perfect geometric array, bushes barbered into inventive shapes, imaginative fountains, and armies of statues. The huge old magnolia trees and orange trees close by relieve some of the formality. Royal guests once entered the garden via the pompous but original **Escadaria dos Leões** (Lions' Staircase). In the early 19th century dozens of live animals — not just dogs, but lions and wolves — were boarded at Queluz, which was then the site of the royal zoo.

Queluz has one rather original attraction, a man-made river. Enclosed between retaining walls covered in precious azulejos, a real stream was actually diverted to pass through the huge palace grounds, and was dammed so the water level could be raised whenever the royal residents wanted a boat ride.

The former royal kitchen has been converted into a prestigious restaurant run by the government-owned *pousada* hotel chain. With giant old utensils, a fireplace big enough for a crowd to walk into, and loads of atmosphere, the place is called,

> Sintra's one-lane entrance road is jammed with waiting cars and tourist buses from 8am to 6pm. It's advisable to take the train from Lisbon so you don't have to worry about parking.

logically, *Cozinha Velha,* "The Old Kitchen."

To get to Queluz, take a bus tour or a commuter train from Rossio station to Queluz. By car it's no more than 20 minutes on the motorway through

the forest of Monsanto; the turn-off on the way to Sintra is clearly signposted. You're hardly out of Lisbon's mushrooming suburbs before you're alongside the elegant palace.

☞ Sintra

Though Sintra suffers the effects of its enduring popularity, it is one of the finest towns in Portugal to visit. Nestled into the Serra de Sintra, 25 km (16 miles) northwest of Lisbon, it was once a coveted summer retreat for royals and today is a romantic getaway for people from all over the world. Clustered throughout the forested hillsides are old palaces and estates with spectacular vistas. Two peaks in the range are crowned by reminders of Sintra's illustrious past: Castelo dos Mouros, the ruins of a castle built by occupying Moors in the 8th century, and Palácio de Pena, the multi-colored fantasy palace built by a German nobleman for his Portuguese wife. The views from either of these points extends as far as the sea, and the entire area, thick with vegetation and paths through the mountain, is spectacular for trekkers.

Right in the center of town is the **Palácio Nacional de Sintra** (also called the *Paço Real,* or "Royal Palace"). Except for its two huge, white conical chimneys, from the outside it looks like a fairly ordinary hulk of a palace. Its real treasures lie inside. A summer home for Portuguese kings

Though the distinctive chimneys of the Palácio Nacional are famous, its interior is the primary attraction.

since the early 14th century, the palace's design became more and more unpredictable and haphazard as wings were added over the centuries, with back-to-back medieval and Manueline style. The resulting interiors and furnishings are remarkable, including some of the oldest and most valuable azulejos in all Portugal.

Every room in the Palácio Nacional has a story to tell. During the 17th century, the dull-witted Afonso VI was pressured into abdicating for the benefit of the country, therefore allowing his more effective brother, Pedro II, to become king. When a plot to restore Afonso to the throne was discovered, the former monarch was exiled to Sintra. For nine years, until he died in 1683, he was imprisoned in a simple room of the Palácio Nacional. It's said that the worn floor is a result of his constant pacing up and down.

A large hall, **Sala das Pegas** (Magpie Salon), tells a very different story. João I (1385–1433) was caught by Queen Philippa — kissing one of her ladies-in-waiting. Palace gossip had a field day until the king ordered the entire ceiling of the hall closed and painted with magpies, as many as there were ladies-in-waiting, their mouths sealed. The royal rebuke, the king's way of saying "so what" and "shut up" had the desired effect.

The so-called **Sala dos Cisnes** (Swan Room) is decorated with ceiling panels painted with swans, each in a different position. There are also precious ceilings with intricate designs in the *mudéjar* style influenced by Moorish art.

The lavish Palácio da Pena in Sintra is a grand and whimsical palace perched on a mountain outside Lisbon.

The odd chimneys, shaped like inverted cones, were used to let the smoke out of the massive kitchen when oxen were being roasted for large banquets given for visiting dignitaries.

A steep road with hairpin turns leads up into the serra from Sintra to the town's most spectacular monuments. The oldest is the **Castelo dos Mouros** (Moors' Castle), which hugs a rocky ridge overlooking the town. It was erected during the eighth century, soon after the Moors occupied Portugal. The dauntless Afonso Henriques conquered it for the Christians in 1147, a major victory in the reconquest of Portugal. Today the castle is a ruin, but a fascinating one, its crenellated walls still severe. Those with the energy to do so should climb the ramparts to the top for incredible views of the entire forested area all the way out to sea and across the tree tops to Sintra's most famous monument, Pena Palace. It's easy to pick out individual *quintas* (estates) in their privileged seclusion.

Farther up the same winding road on the hilltop, the **Palácio da Pena,** more than 450 m (1,500 ft) above sea level, is an outrageous Victorian folly reached by way of a park so lush with flowering trees and vines it resembles a tropical rainforest. In 1511, Manuel I had a monastery built on this site. It was mostly destroyed in the earthquake of 1755, though a notable chapel and cloister survive. The present building is a bizarre and extravagant cocktail of Gothic, Renaissance, Manueline, and Moorish architecture, fashioned as a love nest for Maria II (1834–1853) and her smitten husband, Ferdinand of Saxe-Coburg-Gotha. Few have had the wealth to indulge their free-running fantasies so grandly. Like a child's dream castle, the exterior is a wild, layered construction painted pink, yellow, gray, and red, with crenellated turrets, a studded archway, and monsters guarding doorways. Inside, rooms are chock-full of imaginative, ornate, and, in some cases, suffocatingly sumptuous details. The views from the Disney-esque terraces of the platforms sweep all the way from the Atlantic to Lisbon.

Also located in and around Sintra are: the **Quinta da Regaleira**, a fantastic, turn-of-the-century, turreted mansion, now open to the public at select hours; the **Montserrate Palace Gardens**, wild, lush, and ideal for hiking; the **Palácio de Seteais**, an 18th-century palace, today Sintra's fanciest hotel; the **Museu do Brinquedo**, a 20,000-piece toy museum; and Sintra's **Museum of Modern Art**. A short hop from Sintra are the attractive village of **Colares** and the beach at **Praia das Maçãs**. Sintra's helpful tourist information office, on Praça da República in the old quarter, can direct you to any of these.

Estoril Coast

The Costa do Estoril (formerly called Costa do Sol) begins just west of Lisbon and goes all the way around the tip of the peninsula to Guincho on the open Atlantic. Those seeking pollution-free swimming (see page 87) usually head for Guincho, but the famous old resort of Estoril itself, some 24 km (15 miles) from Lisbon, is still worth a visit.

Sintra's Country Market

On the second and last Sunday of each month, a country fair is held in the adjacent village of São Pedro do Sintra — be prepared for even worse traffic jams than usual. In the open market you can buy homemade bread, cheese, and sausages, or even a bottle of patent medicine sold to you by an old-fashioned, slick-talking hawker. Antiques collectors find many possibilities here, including religious statues, rustic furniture as well as ordinary 19th-century household appliances. The major annual fair is held on 29 June.

The half-hour train journey from Cais do Sodré station in Lisbon to Estoril goes through former fishing villages now turned into soulless commuter suburbs. If you go by the motorway (toll road) you will see nothing of them at all, but the coastal road still provides a scenic drive.

The railway station at **Estoril** is right alongside the beach. On the other side of the tracks (and across the coast road) is a formal park, the front lawn of the town's glitzy **casino**. With its night-club, restaurants, bars, cinema, exhibition halls, shops, and gaming rooms, this is

The Portuguese elite long ago recognized the beauty of the bay of Cascais.

Estoril's one-stop, after-dark amusement center.

In spite of the modern decor, the casino maintains an old-fashioned pace. Gambling is suspended only two nights a year: Good Friday and Christmas Eve. Legend has it that somebody broke the bank one Good Friday, prompting a superstitious management to declare it a holiday thenceforth. (Officials dismiss the story as wishful thinking.)

The rest of Estoril is about as discreet as a Las Vegas high roller. Victorian villas and sleek modern mansions are tucked away behind green curtains of palms, eucalyptus, pines, and vines. In the first half of the 20th century, dignitaries and monarchs, either unexpectedly unemployed or

*Azulejos decorate the town square at Cascais,
and the pavement is an intricate mosaic pattern.*

exiled, gravitated to fashionable Estoril or Cascais and luxurious hideaways.

As early as the mid-18th century, Estoril was attracting visitors because of its balmy climate and thermal spa baths, which were considered good for liver complaints. Long before that, however, prehistoric settlers had built a couple of cave-cemeteries, discovered in 1944 near the beach, dug out of the limestone.

While Estoril is a full-scale resort — cosmopolitan and sybaritic — **Cascais**, which sits on a pretty curved bay, lives a double life. It is a town of both fishermen and kings, where the humble and the retiring rich coexist with camera-toting visitors.

The workaday fishing scene attracts tourists, who inspect the catch as it is unloaded from boats into wooden trays and then rushed to the modern auction building. There the fish are sold by a reverse (Dutch) auction, in which the price starts high and decreases until somebody shouts a bid. You may not understand the chant of the auctioneer, but you'll see what he's selling: lobster, shrimp, hake, squid, and sardines. Retail sales are in the hands of local fishwives, who set up stalls outside the market. For the finished product, try any of the dozen or so restaurants within walking distance of the beach.

The main square is a charmer. The **Paços do Concelho** (Town Hall) has stately windows with iron railings, separated by panels of azulejos depicting saints. The fire station occupies a place of honor between the town hall and an attractive church, while in the main square, with undulating designs in its mosaic pavement, stands a modern statue of Pedro I.

The forbidding 17th-century fort, the **Cidadela** (Citadel), is one of the few buildings to have survived the earthquake and tidal wave of 1755. In a small chapel within the walls is an image of St. Anthony, traditionally borne on the back of a white mule in the parade on the feast day of Santo António (13 June).

After an overdose of sun and salt, the municipal park down the road is a cool relief. Under towering trees, swans preen their feathers alongside ponds brimming with plump red and silver fish. The palace in this park is the **Museu dos Condes de Castro Guimarães**, a museum with archeological remains, art works, old furniture, gold, and silver.

The road west (3 km/2 miles from Cascais) passes **Boca do Inferno** (Mouth of Hell), a geological curiosity where, in rough weather, the waves send up astonishingly high spouts of spray accompanied by ferocious sound effects. On a day when the sea is calm, you'll wonder what all the fuss is about.

At **Guincho**, you have the choice of either a sandy beach or the rocks to fish from, but be careful — they face the open sea and it's often rough. Just up the coast you can see the windswept cape of **Cabo da Roca**, the most westerly point of mainland Europe.

Vacationers to the Costa do Estoril enjoy all the usual sports on land and sea as well as a very sophisticated nightlife. In addition, nowadays there are also some far more specialized events: car racing, theater, a jazz festival, and bullfights. The mean temperature on the coast is mild enough any time of year for a vacation.

South of Lisbon

Arrábida Peninsula

It's around 32 km (20 miles) south from Lisbon over the bridge to the calm and clean seashore at **Sesimbra**. Mornings in this working fishing town the entire adult male population seems to be occupied on or near the beach, taking the knots out of the tough plastic fishing lines or tending to colorful fishing boats. The beach, the main draw for the mostly Portuguese crowd that gathers weekends and holidays, is narrow but quite long, and is sheltered from the brunt of Atlantic tides and harsh winds. Most tourist developments tend to merge fairly unobtrusively into the hillside.

Those castle walls silhouetted on the hilltop above Sesimbra are the genuine article, though recently restored. During the Middle Ages the whole town was situated up there, protected against sea raiders by the walls and the altitude. The Moors built the enclave, lost it to Dom Afonso Henriques in 1165, and won it back again for a few years before having to move out for good in 1200. There's no admittance to the castle, but the

Highlights Outside Lisbon

Palácio Nacional da Pena. Estrada da Pena, Sintra; Tel. 21-923 02 27. Fairytale palace built in 19th century by Ferdinand von Coburg-Gotha for his wife, Maria II. Open Tues–Sun, 10am–5pm (open until 6pm in summer). 600 esc. (free Sun) (See page 58.)

Palácio Nacional de Queluz. Largo do Palácio, Queluz; Tel. 21-435 00 39. Rococo summer palace built by Pedro III for his mad wife, Maria I. Opulent with spectacular gardens. Open Jan–Dec, 10am–5pm; Feb–Apr and Nov, 10am–5pm; May–Oct, 10am–6:30pm. 600 esc.; gardens only, 100 esc. Equestrian show Wed, May–Oct. (See page 56.)

Palácio Nacional de Sintra. Largo Rainha D. Amélia, Sintra; Tel. 21-910 53 40. Sumptuous royal palace with odd conical chimneys and Portugal's most important collection of 15th- and 16th-century azulejos. Open daily, 10am–5pm. 600 esc. (free Sun am). (See page 58.)

Mosteiro de Alcobaça. 100 km (62 miles) north of Lisbon on Hwy. EN 1; Tel. 262-58 39 09. Cistercian abbey founded in 1153 and Portugal's largest church. Open daily: Oct–Mar, 9am–5pm; Apr–Sept, 9am–7pm. 600 esc. (See page 73.)

Mosteiro da Batalha. 120 km (74 miles) north of Lisbon on Hwy. EN 1; Tel. 244-76 54 97. A 14th-century Dominican abbey with a masterful Gothic church and unfinished chapels. Open daily: Oct–Mar 9am–5pm; Apr–Sept, 9am–6pm. 600 esc. (See page 74.)

Óbidos. 98 km (58 miles) north of Lisbon. A perfectly preserved medieval town, still encircled by an unblemished stone wall and crowned by a castle — now a government-run *pousada*.

Estoril coast. 25–35 km (15–20 miles) west of Lisbon. A stretch of fishing villages and chic resorts, including Cascais and Estoril.

A few days in a small coastal town may be the perfect respite from bustling Lisbon.

view down to the curve of the coast and back to the Arrábida mountains is magnificent.

The topographical highlight of the Arrábida peninsula is the **Serra da Arrábida** (site of a nature reserve), a mountain chain around 35 km (22 miles) long that protects the coast from the strong north winds and accounts for the Mediterranean vegetation. The tiny little beach spot **Portinho da Arrábida** is popular with Portuguese weekenders.

Setúbal, the district capital, is a 20-minute drive from Lisbon by motorway, longer if you take the picturesque route via Sesimbra and Arrábida. (The bus does it in an hour; or you can take the ferry across the Tagus and then the slow local train, a total of an hour and a half.) This is olive and citrus country, with cows grazing among the trees. The farther south you go, the more significant the vineyards, with the Setúbal region producing a highly regarded Muscatel.

Setúbal is a conglomeration of market town, industrial center, and resort, and is Portugal's third largest fishing port. Narrow, inviting shopping streets twist through the center of the city.

Setúbal's greatest historical and artistic treasure, the Gothic **Igreja de Jesus**, was built around 1490 by the great French architect Boytac, who later built Lisbon's glorious

Jerónimos Monastery (see page 44). A dramatic main portal leads into the church, which boasts two inspired elements of decoration: 17th-century azulejos on the walls, and stone pillars like twisted strands of clay, fragile-looking in spite of their obviously solid dimensions.

The monastery that adjoins the church has now been converted into the town museum, a mixture of early Portuguese paintings, including a series of the life of Jesus, archeological odds and ends, old furniture and tiles. The cloister was reconstructed after the 1755 earthquake, but since then excavation has revealed parts of the original patio.

The 16th-century, star-shaped fort, high above the town to the west, is now a government-sponsored *pousada* (luxury hotel) with a dreamy sweeping view (see page 134). There's usually some action down in the fishermen's quarter when brightly painted boats of all sizes return with freshly caught fish still wriggling for their lives.

North of Lisbon

North of Lisbon is one of the prettiest sights in Portugal, the walled fortress of Óbidos; the popular seaside and fishing towns of Peniche and Nazaré; and Fátima, a religious shrine for most of the 20th century.

Mafra

In modest Portugal, the dimensions of the convent and palace of Mafra, 40 km (25 miles) to the northwest of Lisbon, are really quite staggering. The frontage of the building, often likened to Spain's Escorial, measures over 220 m (726 ft).

This monumental extravagance is attributable to João V, who in 1711 conceived this project to celebrate the long-awaited birth of his first child, Princess D. Maria, after three years of

The massive interior of the Mafra Complex holds a bevy of marble wonders.

marriage. The project employed as many as 50,000 artists, artisans, and laborers.

The convent **library** is the undisputed highlight; it has a vaulted ceiling, a precious wood floor, and tall shelves housing 30,000 books, making it the largest one-room library in Portugal. The **hospital** is a bizarre church with 16 private sick-rooms lining the nave, so that patients could hear mass from their beds. Visits to the Mafra Palace are by guided tour only (English-speaking tours daily at 11am and 2:30pm; closed Tuesday), and last about an hour.

Another 10 km (6 miles) toward the coast is the fishing village and growing resort of **Ericeira**. The old section is a winsome town of cobbled streets winding between whitewashed cottages, with everything clean, neat, and treasured by both inhabitants and visitors alike.

Ericeira received its town charter around 750 years ago but scarcely attracted any attention until 1910, when Portugal's last king, Manuel II, hastily arrived from Mafra, and in its little port, boarded the royal yacht with his family to sail off into exile.

Óbidos

Almost too perfect to be true, the high medieval walls of **Óbidos** completely encircle a jewel of a town. Equally hard to believe, this inland town was once a port and *coastal* fortress until the sea inlet silted up, leaving the quiet Óbidos lagoon cut off and the shoreline nearly 10 km (6 miles) away.

From the main parking area, you enter the town through a narrow southern gateway, partly lined with azulejos. A second entrance at the north end is guarded by the 13th-century **castle**, with its high square and round towers. It's been adapted as one of the more luxurious and perennially full *pousadas* (see page 134), but even if you aren't staying or eating in the restaurant, you can take a look and enjoy the view from the ramparts.

The narrow streets inside the walls are enchanting, all lined with whitewashed houses decorated with colorful flowers. It's a safe bet that Óbidos has never looked so neat and clean in all its history, and it's inevitably jammed with

A far cry from the Four Seasons, this government-owned pousada was previously the Óbidos castle.

curious visitors at times. To enjoy it without the crowds, stay the night or plan to arrive early or late in the day.

It's a real pleasure just to stroll about, climbing up to and walking along the battlements. Down at street level, Rua Direita, the main drag, runs from one gate to the other. Just down from the castle, the parish church, **Igreja de Santa Maria**, faces the main square. Built on the site of a Visigothic temple and later a mosque, it has handsome, blue 18th-century azulejos, an odd, blue-painted ceiling, and a gilded tomb in the north wall. Afonso V married his cousin Isabel in this small church in 1441, when they were mere children (he was 10, she 8).

In the chapel to the right of the altar, the paintings of the life of St. Catherine are by the Spanish-born Josefa d'Ayala. She came to live in Óbidos, and the Portuguese have adopted her as their own — they usually call her Josefa de Óbidos. She died here in 1684, one of the first women in history to be recognized as a great artist.

Also facing the square is the **municipal museum** in the 16th-century town hall, set up by the Gulbenkian Foundation. Laid out on three levels, a varied collection includes weaponry from the Peninsular War, religious art, and other statuary.

Nearby is the **Igreja da Misericórdia**, a late 15th-century church reputed to be the second alms house established in Portugal.

Peniche

Due west on the coast, the old port of **Peniche** was once an island, but sand gradually accumulated and joined it to the mainland to form the present peninsula. The imposing fortifications, built by Spain during its period of rule in the 16th century, were meant to hold off pirates, or the English (in the time of Sir Francis Drake, they were much the same thing in Spanish eyes).

Fresh seafood is easy to come by in Portuguese restaurants — the fishing ports are active year round.

It's worth collecting a town map at the tourist office, which can also arrange accommodations. You'll find the fishing harbor usually jammed with colorful, storm-battered craft and flanked by some excellent, informal fresh fish restaurants. The fort nearby held political prisoners during the Salazar régime; now it's a museum as well as a display area for local crafts and traditions. The huge sweep of sandy beach facing north is a local favorite. In fine weather you might like to take a trip to the island of **Berlenga**, 12 km (7 miles) offshore. With monastery ruins and an impressive fort which still stands, it's now a sanctuary for seabirds.

Batalha and Alcobaça

Two admirable abbeys are found inland north of Óbidos. The first is Mosteiro de Santa Maria, the former Cistercian monastery at **Alcobaça**. The church is the biggest in Portugal, built to celebrate a victory, the 1147 battle in which Dom

Afonso Henriques took over the town of Santarém from the Moors. Though the exterior of the church has suffered centuries of architectural tinkering, the overall effect is still harmonious.

In the transept, about 30 m (99 ft) apart, are the tombs of Pedro I and his beloved Inês de Castro, their effigies facing each other and surrounded by attendant angels. Pedro and Inês lived a tragic love story that ended with her murder, ordered by Pedro's father, Afonso IV (see page 14). The tombs are decorated with Portugal's greatest medieval stone carving. The delicate sculpture was damaged, though not severely, by French soldiers looking for treasure when they sacked Alcobaça during their 1811 retreat.

The so-called Cloister of Silence, ordered by King Dom Dinis in the early 14th century, is a model of harmony and simplicity. The monastery's 18th-century kitchens have huge tiled fireplaces. River water was channeled directly into the kitchen, so the monks could fill their tea kettles and catch their dinner at the same time.

Farther north (16 km/10 miles) is the many-turreted and buttressed **Mosteiro da Batalha** (Battle Monastery), consecrated to Santa Maria da Vitória. João I ordered the construction of this Gothic masterpiece in gratitude for the victory over Juan I of

The extravagant monastery at Alcobaça is the largest church in Portugal.

Castile in 1385 at the Battle of Aljubarrota, nearby (see page 15). The limestone mass, discolored over time, looks seared at the edges.

In the center of the **Capela do Fundador** (Founder's Chapel), a tomb contains the remains of João and his queen, Philippa of Lancaster; their effigies lie side by side, hand in hand. Niches in the walls hold the tombs of their children, most notably that of Prince Henry the Navigator.

Still on a sepulchral note, Portugal's two Unknown Soldiers are buried in the monastery's **Chapterhouse**. This vaulted chamber, 20 m (66 ft), was a great engineering wonder in its day (c.1400). Due to fears that the unsupported ceiling would collapse at any time, the architect is said to have employed only convicts under sentence of death to work on the project.

The **Claustro Real** (Royal Cloister), like the church, began as a Gothic work, but as construction continued after a couple of centuries the Manueline style was superimposed. The columns and arches are decorated with freewheeling fantasies in delicate filigreed stonework that lightens the cloister's Gothic severity and the rigid geometric design of the gardens. Be sure not to miss the unfinished chapels, open to the sky, at the east end of the church but visited from the outside.

Nazaré

The Portuguese "Nazareth" is probably the fishing village you've seen in pictures. Although a thriving commercial resort now, some fishermen here continue to wear the colorful local dress of black stocking-caps and plaid trousers, and the women still appear in black shawls, bright aprons, and seven petticoats (one for each day of the week). Sadly, few of the traditional wide, flat-bottomed boats are left, and the oxen that once pulled them ashore have gone.

Sítio, the 90 m (297 ft) cliff at the north end of Nazaré, is a supreme vantage point above the green hilly countryside, the tiled roofs of the neatly packed town, and mile after mile of beach open to the full force of the Atlantic Ocean.

In the old town behind the waterfront, many of the white-washed houses have recently been transformed into restaurants, their tables half-blocking the narrow streets. During summer, thousands of tents fill the beaches, providing shade and shelter from the wind for the vacationers.

Fátima

Set in bleak hill country about 135 km (84 miles) north of Lisbon, this fast-growing town of 8,000 people, large

The Pope and the Virgin of Fátima

Pope John Paul II paid his third visit to the shrine of Fátima in May 2000 and beatified (the final step before sainthood) the shepherd boy and girl who claimed to be visited by the Virgin Mary over a period of six months in 1913 (and died shortly thereafter). It is the first beatification by the Church of children that were not martyrs.

The Pope cites a personal connection to Fátima, crediting the Virgin of Fátima with intervening and protecting him in a 1981 assassination attempt that occurred on May 13, the anniversary of the first apparition of the Virgin. One of the two bullets that struck the pope was placed in the crown of the statue of the Virgin at Fátima.

The Virgin is said to have disclosed three secrets, or prophecies, to the children. After the pope's most recent visit, the Vatican revealed that the "Third Secret of Fátima" prophesied the assassination attempt on Pope John Paul and the persecution of Christians in the 20th century by communist regimes. Only two of the three secrets — a vision of Hell, thought by most to mean World War II, and the rise and fall of Soviet Communism — previously had been made public.

apartment blocks, and countless hotels was once just a poor village. For years, though, it has claimed its place as one of the most important centers of pilgrimage in the Catholic world, along with Lourdes in France and Santiago de Compostela in Spain. Outside of scheduled pilgrimages, which often feature incredible displays of devotion, the shrine is of interest primarily to those visiting for religious reasons.

The 20th-century Neo-Baroque basilica faces an immense but rather plain square, said to be twice as big as St. Peter's in Rome. On 13 May 1917, three young shepherds claimed they saw a series of miraculous visions of the Virgin Mary, followed by a solar phenomenon witnessed by thousands in October of the same year. Francisco and Jacinta, the two younger shepherds, died of pneumonia soon after these inexplicable events. Lucia, the oldest, who was 10 or 11 years old at the time, is now in her 90s, and has been a cloistered Carmelite nun in Coimbra since 1929. She makes very few public appearances now, although she received communion from Pope John Paul II during his May 2000 visit to Fátima.

Pilgrimages are held on the 13th of every month, with the most important observances on that date in May and October. Yet even on an ordinary weekday, scattered believers, some kneeling in penitence, come to Fátima to pay homage to the Virgin Mary.

Pilgrims come from the world over to light candles at the Fátima shrine.

WHAT TO DO

SHOPPING

Lisbon is growing more and more cosmopolitan, but it hasn't lost its old-fashioned feel and its traditional crafts. There are both chic boutiques and outdoor markets here, and you can buy everything from expensive and intricate works of gold and silver to handcrafts that have been produced for hundreds of years, like the classic wool Arraiolos rugs.

Best Buys

Handicrafts especially excel in Portugal. **Azulejos**, the hand-painted ceramic tiles that have been decorating Portugal's walls throughout the centuries, are one of the top crafts. You can buy a scene on a single blue-and-white tile, an address plaque for your house, or a batch to assemble into a picture when you get home. Some shops will paint tiles to order if you have a particular design in mind, and some will copy a photograph. Delicate Portuguese **embroidery** and **lacework**, especially that produced by women on the island of Madeira, is excellent. Hand-embroidered goods also come from the Azores and some mainland towns, notably Viana do Castelo.

Filigree work, a legacy of the Moors, is of extremely high quality. Look for silver filigree earrings and brooches, often in the form of flowers or butterflies. Portuguese **pottery** and **ceramics** are found in many different designs and colors, from fine porcelain to folksy earthenware. Hand-painted wood or ceramic brightly colored **roosters** are popular with many visitors.

Arraiolos, an Alentejo village, has been producing fine **wool rugs** in bright colors and cheerful designs for three centuries. **Hand-woven baskets**, which differ by region, are strong, utilitarian, and often very pretty. As a bonus, they can carry other purchases home. Varied items made from **cork** are typical; Portugal is the world's leading producer of cork, and not only for those millions of wine bottles.

Speaking of wine, Portugal has long been famous for its fortified **port wine** from the Douro Valley near Oporto in the north. Best known as an after-dinner tradition, it also comes in apéritif versions (see page 98). Vintage port of the most select years is what connoisseurs and collectors seek, but there are more accessible ports to take home. Look for aged tawnys, LBV (late bottle vintages), or, for something a little more unusual, a bottle of white port.

> The Lisboa Shopping Card offers discounts from 5–20 percent at shops in Baixa, Chiado, and Av. Liberdade. The card is available in 24- and 72-hour versions from Turismo de Lisboa offices.

Madeira wine, from the volcanic soil of the Portuguese island out in the Atlantic, is served either before or after dinner, as a dessert wine. While these regional wines get most of the attention, Portugal also produces a number of excellent red and white table wines, which make good gifts and souvenirs. Look for those from Dão and Alentejo, as well as *vinhos verdes* (young wines) from Minho. Given their weight and bulk, it's often best to wait until the duty-free shop at the airport.

To enjoy the sounds of Portugal back home, take home a classic **fado recording**, perhaps by Amália Rodrigues or Carlos Paredes, or a disc of ethereal Portuguese **pop** by the Lisbon group Madredeus.

Antiques collectors often browse in the shops in Rua Dom Pedro V, the bustling street descending from the Rato to Cais do Sodré, and Rua de São José in the district called Graça.

Much of the **clothing** you'll see in Lisbon comes from international store chains, though a number of **high fashion** de-

signers from Portugal — such as Ana Salazar and Fátima Lopes — are gaining international attention. Hand-knitted pullovers in sophisticated designs or chunky fishermen's sweaters from Nazaré are good buys.

Leather belts, bags, and shoes are very popular buys. Shoes are just about as fashionable as in Spain and Italy, and even cheaper.

When and Where to Shop

Most shops are open Monday–Friday from 9am–1pm and from 3pm–7pm; Saturday from 9am–1pm. Modern shopping malls are usually open from

The Caldas de Reinha market has a wealth of treasures to admire or purchase.

10am– midnight or later, and sometimes on Sunday. Some of the Baixa shops stay open during lunchtime.

Principal shopping areas include **Baixa's** Avenida da Liberdade, Rua Aurea, and Rua da Prata; and **Chiado**, especially the Armazens do Chiado mall and Rua Garrett.

Markets are fun for their atmosphere as much as the goods for sale. Behind São Vicente de Fora church, in the Campo de Santa Clara, a market (known as *Feira da Ladra* or "Thieves' Market") is held on Tuesday and Saturday. On the fringes of the kitchenware and workaday clothing stalls are dusty treasures and an incredible range of second-hand items.

Across the street under an Indian-looking dome is Lisbon's lively main market, the **Mercado da Ribeira,** where more than a thousand people work.

> *Quánto custa?*
> How much is it?
> *Tem maior/mais pequeno?*
> Do you have a larger/ smaller one?

Men in padded caps balance unwieldy wicker trays of fruit and vegetables on their heads, and the scent of fresh corian-der pervades the air. Since it is both a wholesale and retail market, there is always something interesting going on, from 2am to 9pm. The best time to absorb the colorful atmosphere is just before lunch, when you can pick up the makings for a great picnic, too.

The vast **country market** in Sintra is held on the second and fourth Sunday of each month. Sintra, so popular with for-eign visitors, has a wealth of shops for its small size, many of them specializing in ceramics, pottery, and antiques.

Note: you may get away with haggling at antiques stalls in the flea market, but it's not worth trying anywhere else.

ENTERTAINMENT

The Portuguese capital has a wide variety of nightlife options, and hot new clubs and bars are springing up in the newly renovated areas along the River Tagus.

The IVA Tax

For non-EU residents, the IVA tax (Value Added Tax) imposed on most goods can be refunded on purchases of at least 11,700 esc. in a single store. Look for the blue-and-white TAX FREE sign in stores. To obtain the rebate, simply fill in a form provided by the shop where you purchase the goods. One copy is kept by the shop; the others must be presented at customs upon de-parture. The refund can be credited back to your credit card at the airport or mailed to your home address after your return.

Nightclubs, Bars, and Live Music. The classic nighttime outing in Lisbon is still to the *fado* houses in Alfama or Bairro Alto. A century ago, "respectable" people were reluctant to be seen in a *fado* club; nowadays the danger is not to your reputation, only to your wallet, as tickets are quite expensive. Many offer dinner as well as drinks. Inclusive tours are available.

In Lisbon's Bairro Alto you can also find conventional discos, nightclubs, jazz clubs and bars for all tastes, some open until 5am. Clubs to consider include: Adega Machado (Rua do Norte, 91; Tel. 21-322 46 40; Metro: Chiado); A Parreirinha da Alfama (Beco do Espírito Santa, 1; Tel. 21-886 82 09); Lisboa à Noite (Rua das Gáveas, 69; Tel. 21-346 02 22); Luso (Travessa da Queimada, 10; Tel. 21-342 22 81;

Fado

Fado, the soulful Portuguese song — literally "fate, translated into music" — is based on a story or poem, and accompanied by a 12-string guitar. The dramatic atmosphere of a fado house adds to the occasion. Guitarists start off the proceedings with a warm-up number. The lights dim, the audience goes quiet, and a spotlight picks out a woman in black who begins to wail out a song of tragedy and despair. Her sultry voice sums up that most Portuguese emotion, *saudade* — a swell of longing, regret, and nostalgia. Though most often characterized by melancholy or despair, there are also joyful and relatively upbeat fados.

Most *fado* singers are women, but you are also likely hear a man perform the same sort of ballad with a strong, husky voice. The *fado* is much too solemn to be danced. Instead, regional fishermen's and shepherds' dances are sometimes performed to perk things up.

The highly emotional fado performance delves into the hardships and heartbreaks of Portuguese life.

Metro: Chiado); A Severa (Rua das Gáveas, 51; Tel. 21-342 83 14); Senyor Vinho (Rua do Meio à Lapa; Tel. 21-397 26 81; Metro: Avenida).

Concerts and Dance. Lisbon's cultural scene offers occasional opera, symphony concerts, ballet, and recitals, usually held in winter. The city's opera company is well regarded, and the Gulbenkian Foundation (see page 48) maintains its own symphony orchestra and ballet company.

Portugal has three other important symphony orchestras and a national dance company. Soloists and ensembles from many countries also perform here.

Venues include: Coliseu dos Recreios (Rua das Portas de Santo Antão, 96; Tel. 21-324 05 80), a circular construction and the second-largest music and events hall in Lisbon; Atlântico Hall (Parque das Nações; Tel. 21-891 93 33;

A display of folkloric dancing is one of the rich cultural traditions that visitors can enjoy while visiting Lisbon.

<www.parquedasnacoes.pt>), the place for big-time rock bands and Brazilian acts; Fundação Calouste Gulbenkian (Av. de Berna, 45; Tel. 21-793 51 31), which hosts varied recitals, classical music, and dance programs, including open-air concerts in summer; Teatro Nacional de São Carlos (Rua Serpa Pinto, 9; Tel. 21-346 59 14) is Lisbon's opera house; and Centro Cultural de Belém (Praça do Império; Tel. 21-361 24 00), which has a wide program of cultural performances.

Theater and Cinema. Most of Lisbon's stage plays are comedies and revues — in Portuguese, of course. The best-known theater is **Teatro Nacional de Dona Maria II** (Praça de Dom Pedro IV/Rossio; Tel. 21-342 22 46).

Cinemas tend to show foreign films in the original language with Portuguese subtitles. An old-style, 1950s movie house with large screen is **São Jorge** (Av. Liberdade, 175; Tel. 21-357 91 44).

Gambling. The **Estoril Casino** (Tel. 21-468 45 21; see page 63) is the big draw for gamblers. To enter the gaming rooms you have to pay a fee and show your passport. The casino is open daily 3pm–3am (closed Good Friday and Christmas Eve). A sign suggests that gentlemen wear jackets after 8pm, but no rules are enforced.

> The local publications *What's On in Lisbon*, the weekly *Sete*, and the monthly *Agenda Cultural* contain the most complete music, stage, and screen listings, including times of performances.

Festivals

Portugal's folk festivals are modest compared with such international attractions as the Carnival in Rio or the running of bulls in Pamplona. Tourist information offices have a timetable of festivals and fairs around the country, which is worth checking as you plan your excursions.

Most colorful religious processions are confined to the north of the country. In towns around Lisbon, Patron Saint's Days may be celebrated both at church and with dancing in the streets, fireworks, and bullfights.

Carnival time in Lisbon is a rather subdued affair. Firecrackers go off in the streets, but pre-Lenten festivities on the whole tend to be confined to private parties. The beach resort Nazaré, north of Lisbon, celebrates with a bit more style.

The date of the year's first pilgrimage to Fátima, 13 May, is perennially a big event. June is the month of Lisbon's popular saints (Festa dos Santos Populares): António (Anthony), João (John), and Pedro (Peter). Fairs are held in the neighborhoods with folk dancing, sports competitions, and exciting firework displays. The biggest day is 13 June, honoring the local boy who grew up to be St. Anthony of Padua (see page 30).

During the second half of July, Estoril celebrates its annual classical music festival.

SPORTS

From swimming and hiking to the challenge of deep-sea fishing, sports enthusiasts have plenty of options in the Lisbon area. The temperate climate also means year-round golf and tennis.

If you're interested in diving or water skiing, or any other sport for which you need to hire equipment, ask at the tourist information offices in each town about the best places to do so.

Active Sports

Diving. Just off Sesimbra, south of Lisbon, the extraordinarily clear, calm waters are considerably good for snorkeling and scuba diving.

Fishing. All along the coast you will see anglers in boots casting off from the beaches, and others perched on rocks or man-made promontories. The best deep-sea fishing is for swordfish around Sesimbra.

Golf. The Lisbon area has several courses, including: top-rated Estoril Golf Club (18 holes) at Estoril, Tel. 21-468 01 76; Golf Estoril Sol (9 holes) near Sintra, Tel. 21-923 24 61; Lisbon Sports Club at Belas (18 holes) near Queluz, Tel. 21-431 00 77; and Quinta da Marinha Golf and Country Club (18 holes), designed by Robert Trent Jones Sr., near Cascais, Tel. 21-486 98 81.

Riding. You can hire a horse, with or without an instructor, at the Lisbon Country Club or at the Quinta da Marinha Golf and Country Club, which also has an equestrian center; Tel. 21-486 92 82. In Sintra, several of the upscale hotels, including Palácio de Seteais and Quinta da Capela (see pages 132–133), offer horseback riding through local operators.

Sailing and Boating. Most beaches protected from the open ocean have row boats, canoes, or pedalos for rent by the hour. Experienced sailors in search of a more seaworthy craft should ask at the local yacht marina. Rowboats are also available at Parque das Nações near the Oceanário.

Swimming. Because of pollution along the Estoril Coast, you should not swim any closer to Lisbon than at Estoril itself, which has been granted an EU blue flag. At Guincho and beyond the sea is perfectly clean and quite safe for swimming, but beware of the strong undertow. South of Lisbon from Caparica onwards is delightful, but can also be windy, with very rough seas.

Ask at the government tourist office for the leaflet on Portuguese beaches, with maps and details of facilities.

Tennis. Major hotels tend to have their own tennis courts, but there are tennis clubs and public courts as well. The Tivoli Lisboa in Lisbon is one of the rare city hotels with tennis courts on the premises. Many golf clubs also have their own courts.

Spectator Sports

Bullfights. The Portuguese bullfight, known as *Arte Marialva*, is a tradition dating to the 16th century. It is less conclusive than the Spanish version — since the 18th century, it has been forbidden to kill the bulls. Still, many will still find the spectacle to be anything but art or sport. Eight bulls, each weighing nearly half a ton, enter the arena in turn. Four are fought *à antiga portuguesa*, in the uniquely Portuguese way, and four are taken on by a matador who dominates the bull with his cape, without killing the bull and without the

The Portuguese bullfight is more pageantry than battle; unlike its Spanish cousin, the bull is spared his life.

aid of picadors. The four rounds *à antiga* are equal parts circus, horse-show, and rodeo.

Lisbon's **Campo Pequeno Praça de Touros** bullring (Tel. 21-793 24 42; Metro: Campo Pequeno), at the top of Avenida da República, is a Victorian red-brick landmark with mock-Moorish arches and bulbous domes. The **Monumental** arena in Cascais is bigger, but a bullfighter hasn't made it until he conquers the fans at Campo Pequeno.

The season runs from Easter Sunday to October. As in Spain, seats in the shade (*sombra*) cost more than in the sun (*sol*), though there are performances in the evening as well. For a modicum of comfort, rent a pillow from the usher.

Car Racing. The Formula One Grand Prix takes place at Estoril's autodrome, on the road to Sintra, in late September.

Football (Soccer). As in most countries, this usually draws big crowds in Portugal. Lisbon's two major teams are Benfica, which plays at Estádio da Luz, and Sporting Clube de Portugal, which holds matches at Estádio do José Alvalade near Campo Grande.

CHILDREN'S LISBON

With its trams, elevators, funiculars, and ferries, Lisbon offers some great ways to entertain the kids just by touring around the city or crossing the River Tagus. The Transtejo ferry that traverses the breadth of the city along the river lasts a full two hours, so some younger kids might get restless.

The biggest new attraction in Lisbon for children is the **Parque das Nações** (see page 52), with its splendid aquarium (Oceanário de Lisboa; Tel. 21-891 70 02), playgrounds, fountains, paddleboats, and aerial cable cars. The **Planetário Calouste Gulbenkian** (Praça do Império in Belém; Tel. 21-362 00 02) has special planetarium shows for children on Sunday mornings.

North of the aqueduct, **Jardim Zoológico de Lisboa** (Zoo, Estada de Benfica, 58; Tel. 21-726 93 49; Metro: Jardim Zoológico) is old-fashioned but makes an effort to entertain younger visitors with features such as elephant rides, boats, and a miniature train. It's in a nice park, but the animals don't have much room to move about.

Campo Grande, situated between the zoo and the airport, is a popular park with Lisboêtas and visitors alike. Palm, cedar, and willow trees shade pretty walks and a small lake with rowing boats.

For a safe beach with clean water you'll have to travel some way from the city (see page 87). Head for Guincho and Caparica when the wind is light, or Sesimbra and Tróia otherwise. Caparica has a waterpark with long, twisting slides.

Calendar of Events

As you plan your excursions, it is worth checking details of festivals and fairs around the country with tourist information offices.

February *Lisbon*: Fado Festival at various sites in Lisbon.

February–March Carnival (Mardi Gras). Processions and nightly fireworks.

March–April Holy Week. Palm Sunday, Good Friday, and Easter Day services and processions.

May *Sesimbra*: Festival of Senhor das Chagas procession (3–5 May). *Fátima*: First Pilgrimage, 13 May. *Lisbon*: Bullfights at Campo Pequeno (every Thurs through Sept).

June *Lisbon*: Festival of music, dance and theater (all month). *Lisbon and elsewhere* (especially Alfama): Fairs and festivities honoring St. Anthony (13th), St. John (24th) and St. Peter (29th).

July *Sintra*: Music Festival, including live performances in the town's historic palaces and gardens (second week). *Vila Franca de Xira* (north of Lisbon): Running of bulls in the streets (first two Sun).

July–August *Estoril/Cascais*: Estoril International Music Festival. *Estoril and Cascais*: Open-air craft fair every evening. *Cascais*: Cascais Jazz Festival (first two weekends). *Setúbal*: Festival of Santiago, fair and exhibition.

August *Peniche*: Festival of Our Lady of the Good Voyage. *Sintra*: Ballet Festival at Hotel de Seteais.

September *Palmela*: Wine Festival, parades, tastings and fireworks (mid-Sept). *Nazaré*: Festival of Our Lady (second week). *Cabo Espichel*: Festival of Our Lady of the Cape (last Sun).

October *Estoril*: Estoril Open Golf Tournament. *Vila Franca de Xira*: Fair, running of bulls (first Sun). *Fátima*: Pilgrimage (13th). *Óbidos*: Early Music Festival (second week).

November *Lisbon*: ATP Tour Masters Tennis World Championship tournament.

December *Lisbon*: Bolsa de Natal Christmas market (throughout city).

EATING OUT

Seafood fans are in luck in Lisbon, with a surfeit of just-caught fish and shellfish. Not that restaurants skimp on meat: you can find delicious pork and lamb dishes and steak. More adventurous palates can try cuisines imported from Portugal's former African and Asian colonies. You'll also enjoy freshly picked fruit and vegetables, not to mention Portuguese wines, which are eminently drinkable.

Portions in Portuguese restaurants tend to be rather large. You can ask for a half portion (which is usually charged at around two-thirds the full price).

Restaurants and Menus

Government inspectors rate all Portuguese restaurants in four categories or *classe*. In descending order the classes are: *luxo* (luxury), *primeira* (first), s*egunda* (second) , and *terceira* (third). The scale is as much as anything an indicator of how costly a meal is likely to be. A rating sign is often displayed outside restaurants, while menus shown in the window or beside the door let you know what to expect in variety and price. Prices normally include taxes and a service charge, but you are expected to leave an additional 5 to 10 percent tip for good service.

Whether you indulge in one of Lisbon's chic new riverfront restaurants or absorb some local color in a humble fishermen's hangout (where you'll often find the best food), you are likely to come across a variety of dishes and preparations entirely new to you.

The Tourist Menu and Other Cautionary Tales

Many restaurants and cafés offer an *ementa turística* — literally a "tourist menu." However, the term does not connote a poor-grade meal of easily identifiable international fare, targeting tourists who'll never again set foot in the restaurant. Rather, it is an economically priced set meal — typically bread, butter, soup, main course, and dessert.

The prices displayed outside some of Lisbon's cafés may apply only if you stand at the bar. In Portugal, as in some other European countries, if you sit down at a table, you will have to pay the higher prices quoted on the regular menu. Also, in restaurants where seafood portions are charged by weight, waiters may bring out repeated portions without your specifically ordering more. If you don't refuse them early on, the bill might be quite a shock.

Mealtimes

Breakfast (*pequeno almoço*) is usually eaten any time up until about 10am. **Lunch** (*almoço*) is served from shortly after noon until 3pm, and **dinner** (*o jantar*) runs from 7:30 to 9:30pm (or later in a *casa de fado*). Snacks between meals are usually taken at a *pastelaria* (pastry and cake shop), *salão de chá* (tea shop), or what the Portuguese call, in English, a *snack bar* — a stand-up counter selling sandwiches, savory pastries, and sweets.

Because lunch and dinner tend to be major events, you may prefer the kind of light breakfast the Portuguese eat: coffee, toast or rolls, butter and jam. Hotels usually provide all the extras — juice, cereal, eggs, bacon — in large American-style buffets.

Nearly every restaurant in Portugal serves a *couvert* — an assortment of appetizers, including bread and butter, that appear to be free but are usually not. You will be charged anywhere from 100 to 800 esc. for the items. If you do not touch them, however, in theory you should not be charged for them. You will probably have to point this out; few people opt to abstain.

Local Specialties

Soups. Lunch and dinner often get off to a hearty start, and soups are typical Portuguese fare. *Caldo verde* (green soup) is a thick broth of potato purée with finely-shredded cabbage or kale. Sometimes sausage is added. *Sopa à Portuguesa* is similar to *caldo verde*, but

> Salt and pepper are seldom placed on the table. You will be given them if you ask, though: *Sal e pimenta, faz favor*.

with added broccoli, turnips, beans, carrots, and anything else the cook happens to have on hand. *Sopa de cozido* is a rich meat broth with cabbage and perhaps macaroni added. (This course is often followed by *cozido*, a huge serving of all the things that were boiled to create the broth, including beef, chicken, pork, sausages, potatoes, cabbage, and carrots.) *Canja de galinha* is simple chicken-and-rice soup.

Seafood. The best advertisement for seafood is usually the window of a restaurant: a generous refrigerated display case with crabs and prawns, oysters and mussels, sea bass, and sole. Seafood restaurants generally sell shellfish by the weight, giving the price in escudos per kilo. You may wish to have a calculator handy, or be sure they give you the price in easier-to-calculate euros. The Portuguese are very fond of boiled fish dishes, usually served with generous portions of cabbage and boiled potatoes and doused with a little oil and vinegar.

A number of seafood dishes are true local specialties. *Caldeirada* is a rich seafood stew. *Amêijoas na cataplana* is an invention from the Algarve, of steamed mussels (or clams) with sausages, tomato, white wine, ham, onion, and herbs. *Açorda de marisco* is a spicy, garlic-scented thick bread-soup full of seafood bits; raw eggs are later added into the mixture. *Lulas recheadas* are squid stuffed with rice, olives, tomato, onion, and herbs. *Lampreia à Minho* is lamprey, not always highly re-garded, but quite a delicacy in Portugal, served with a bed of rice and red wine sauce (best from January to March). *Sardinhas* (sardines) are excellent and often served grilled (*sardinhas assadas*). *Bacalhau* (cod) is the national dish of Portugal, even

> A menu that quotes a price as "preço V" (or simply "PV"), usually for seafood or shellfish, means variable, i.e. market, price. It is wise to clarify the day's market price before ordering.

though it can be expensive and comes dried and salted and from distant seas.

The Portuguese say that cod is served in 100, 365, or 1,000 different ways (depending on the teller's taste for hyperbole). For many people, *bacalhau* is an acquired taste. For those unconvinced of its attributes, the best way to try it is in *Bacalhau à Gomes de Sá*, in which flaky chunks are baked with parsley, potatoes, onion and olives and garnished with grated hard-boiled egg.

Fresh fish, whole or filleted, is usually served grilled, as are outstanding *atum* (tuna) and *espadarte*, swordfish steaks. For those who know some Spanish or Portuguese, *peixe espada* might sound like swordfish; however, it is actually scabbard fish, a long, thin fish that comes from the area south of Lisbon.

Meat. *Bife na frigideira* is not what you might think. *Frigideira* means frying pan, and this dish is a beefsteak nicely done in a wine sauce. *Cabrito assado* is baked kid served with rice and potato, heavy going but delicious. *Carne de porco à Alentejana* is an inspired dish of clams and pork cooked with paprika and garlic. *Espetada mista* means Portuguese shish kebab: chunks of beef, lamb and pork on a spit. *Feijoada* is the national dish of Brazil, the former Portuguese colony. In Portugal, it's not nearly as elaborate or ritualized, but it's still a hearty and tasty stew of pigs' feet and sausage, white beans, and cabbage.

Most meat dishes are served with *both* rice and potatoes.

Game and Fowl. *Frango* (chicken) is popular and prepared many ways: stewed in wine sauce, fried, roasted, and barbecued to a tasty crisp. Some restaurants specialize in game — *codorniz* (quail), *perdiz* (partridge), *lebre* (hare) and even *javali* (wild boar).

Dessert and Cheese. The Portuguese sweet tooth may be a little too much for your taste. Locals pour sugar on a sliced sweet orange, after all. The cakes, custards, and pastries are usually made with the basics, egg yolks and sugar, and are delicious. *Pudim flã* (also *flam*, *flan*, or *flão*) is the Portuguese version of the Spanish *flan* (caramel custard). *Arroz doce* is rice pudding with a

Café "A Brasiliera" in the Chiado district is a charming spot to chat with friends.

dash of cinnamon. *Maçã assada* is a tasty sugary baked apple. *Pudim Molotov* sounds like a bomb, and indeed it's so rich that it's sure to explode any strict diet. The fluffy egg-white mousse is immersed in a sticky caramel sauce.

For those whose waistlines are wary of such indulgence, there's always cheese. The richest and most expensive in Portugal is *Serra da Estrela*, a delicious cured ewe's milk cheese that originates high up in the mountains. Also on many menus is *Flamengo*, a mild cheese very similar to Edam. Some restaurants serve *queijo fresco* as an appetizer.

This is a small, white, soft mini-cheese made of ewe's and goat's milk, and is so bland that you'll want to add pepper and salt.

International and Exotic Cuisine

Thanks to Portugal's imperial legacy, you can experiment while you're in Lisbon. The former colony of Goa accounts for the local popularity of *caril* (curry) and other Indian-style dishes. A typical Goan delicacy, a lot less pungent than Indian food, is *xacuti* (pronounced and sometimes spelled *chacuti*).

The Port in Portugal...

Thanks to the unique growing conditions of the Douro Valley in the north of Portugal, fortified port wine has tantalized palates around the world since the British began exporting it in the 17th century. It differs from other wines due to the microclimate and soil of the region, and to the fact that the fermentation process is stopped with brandy.

Around 10 percent of the grapes picked each year are still crushed in treading rooms by barefoot men. After two or three days' fermentation the brandy is added. The following spring, the fortified wine is sent to mature at the lodges on the banks of the River Douro at Vila Nova de Gaia (opposite Porto), from where it is shipped.

...and Madeira from Madeira

First produced on the island of Madeira in the 15th century, Madeira wine became an important export trade due to a combination of its notable quality and Madeira's position on the shipping lanes to the Indies. With the rise of the British colonies in North America and the West Indies, it fast became a favorite on both sides of the Atlantic.

Madeira wine only became a fortified wine when it was decided to add grape brandy in order to stabilize it on long sea voyages.

The dish is simply chunks of fried chicken in a sauce of pepper, coriander, saffron, cinnamon, cumin, anise, cloves, and coconut milk served with steamed rice.

> A bottle of vintage port should be consumed within 48 hours of opening. At home or in Portugal, don't pay big bucks for a glass of a rare vintage port unless the bartender opens the bottle in front of you. For most establishments, that's too expensive a proposition.

Piri-piri is a hot-pepper condiment and preparation from Angola that will set most mouths ablaze. Order a piri-piri dish with extreme caution.

Four centuries of ties with the territory of Macau assures all lovers of Chinese food a night out with dishes such as *gambas doces* (sweet-and-sour prawns) and all the fixings.

Drinks: Table Wines

Portuguese wines, while not as well known as those from Spain and France, across the board are quite good, and several regions produce truly excellent wines. You need do nothing more than tell the waiter *tinto* (red) or *branco* (white), and you can't go wrong.

Vinho verde (green wine), produced in the northwest, is a young white wine, slightly fizzy, light, and delightful. A lesser-known type is red wine from the same region, bearing the seemingly oxymoronic name *vinho verde tinto* (red green wine). Both of these wines should be served chilled, as should Portuguese rosé, which is also slightly bubbly and may be either sweet or very dry. *Vinhos maduros* are mature, or aged, wines.

Vinho espumante is Portuguese sparkling wine, packaged in a Champagne-shaped bottle. Most are sweet but you can also find some quite dry versions.

Several of the best wine-producing regions have names whose use is controlled by law (*região demarcada*). You may come across these classifications: Bucelas, a light and fresh white wine; Colares, a traditional red wine; and Setúbal, a mellow, sweet white, sometimes served as an apéritif.

Dão and Douro in the north of Portugal produce vigorous reds and flavorful whites. Wines from the Alentejo region are also highly regarded.

The two most celebrated Portuguese wines, port and Madeira, are mostly known as dessert wines, but they may also be sipped as apéritifs. The before-dinner varieties are dry or extra dry white port and the dry Madeiras, *Sercial* and *Verdelho*. These should be served slightly chilled. After dinner, sip one of the famous ruby or tawny ports (aged tawnys are especially good), or a Madeira dessert wine, *Boal* or *Malvasia* (Malmsey).

Other Drinks

Portuguese beers are good and refreshing. Light or dark, they are served chilled, bottled, or from the tap. One of the best and most common is Sagres. *Aguardente* (literally "fire water") is the local brandy.

Coffee and Tea

At the end of lunch or dinner, most people order a *bica*, a small cup of black espresso coffee — also called simply *um café* or *um café espresso*.

Tea (chá, pronounced "shah") remains a very popular drink in Portugal — after all, it was the Portuguese explorers who first introduced it to the rest of the Western world. Although the concept of afternoon tea is regarded as British, its origins are in fact Portuguese, dating from 1662, when Catherine of Bragança, sister of Dom Afonso VI, married the English King Charles II. Her fashionable court popularized tea drinking.

Menu Reader

To Help You Order ...

Could we have a table?	**Queremos uma mesa.**		
Do you have a set-price menu?	**Tem uma ementa turística?**		
I'd like a/an/some ...		**Queria ...**	
beer	**uma cerveja**	mineral water	**água mineral**
the bill	**a conta**	napkin	**guardanapo**
bread	**pão**	salad	**salada**
butter	**manteiga**	salt	**sal**
dessert	**sobremesa**	sandwich	**sanduíche**
fish	**peixe**	soup	**sopa**
fruit	**fruta**	sugar	**açúcar**
ice-cream	**gelado**	tea	**chá**
meat	**carne**	vegetables	**legumes**
menu	**a carta**	wine	**vinho**
milk	**leite**	wine list	**carta de vinhos**

... and Read the Menu

alho	garlic	**lombo**	fillet
ameijoas	baby clams	**lulas**	squid
arroz	rice	**mariscos**	shellfish
assado	roast	**mexilhões**	mussels
bacalhau	codfish	**ovo**	egg
besugo	sea bream	**ostras**	oysters
dobrada	tripe	**pescada**	hake
dourada	sea-bass	**pescadinha**	whiting
feijões	beans	**polvos**	baby octopus
frito	fried	**queijo**	cheese
gambas	prawns	**salmonete**	red mullet
lagosta	spiny lobster	**truta**	trout
lenguado	sole	**vitela**	veal

HANDY TRAVEL TIPS

An A–Z Summary of Practical Information

A

ACCOMMODATIONS (See also CAMPING on page 103, YOUTH HOSTELS on page 126 and RECOMMENDED HOTELS on page 127)
Except for family-run *hotéis rurais,* hotels in Portugal are graded from 2-star to 5-star deluxe. The rates are lower in less elaborate hostelry: an *estalagem* or inn; a *pensão* (rooms with meals available); or *residencial* (rooms, generally without meals). Confusingly, even some elite, intimate inns in Lisbon are often referred to as a *pensão.*

Pousadas (like Spanish *paradors*) are state-run establishments usually in historic buildings and scenic sites, aimed at acquainting visitors with traditions in different parts of the country. Special attention is given to local food and wine as well as to the architecture and handicrafts of the region. Ask at tourist offices (see page 124) for a detailed list, or see the web site, <www.pousadas.pt>.

When you arrive at your accommodation, you'll usually be asked for your passport and to sign a form which sets out the conditions, prices, and room number. Breakfast may be included in the total cost.

a double/single room   **um quarto duplo/simples**

with/without bath   **com/sem banho**

AIRPORT (*Aeroporto*)
The Aeroporto de Lisboa is only 4 miles from the city center, a 15-minute drive (allow twice as long at rush hour). There is a helpful tourist information office on hand.

Bus 91, the AeroBus airport shuttle, leaves about every 20 minutes, 7am–9pm. The shuttle passes through the city center, including the Rossio, on the way to Cais do Sodré train station. The ticket (460 esc.) can be used all day on trams and buses (though not the Metro subway). Taxis are plentiful (see page 121) and charge about 2,000 esc. to the center of Lisbon.

Lisbon

The main airport number is Tel. 21-848 11 01. For information on flight times call Tel. 21-840 20 60; for airport information, call Tel. 21-840 22 62.

The AeroBus shuttle also picks up passengers at selected hotels throughout Lisbon. Call Tel. 96-629 85 58 to schedule a pick-up, or check with the tourist information office to see if your hotel is one of those designated for pick-ups.

Where do I get the bus to the airport/to the center of Lisbon?	**Onde posso apanhar o autocarro para o aeroporto/ para o centro da cidade?**

B

BUDGETING FOR YOUR TRIP

Airport transfer: The shuttle bus service costs 460 esc.; a taxi will cost about 2,000–2,500 esc.

Accommodations. Hotels in Lisbon are the most expensive in Portugal, and at top levels compare to other large European cities. Still, there are some good values to be found. A 2-star hotel should run 12,000 esc. or less for a double; a 3-star hotel 12,000–20,000 esc., and for a 4-star hotel, expect to pay up to 35,000 esc. Government-owned pousadas are usually priced like 4-star hotels, though the most in-demand historic ones may go higher. Keep in mind that most prices do not include breakfast or the 17% IVA tax.

Car rental. Prices for a subcompact, 4-door car with manual transmission, air conditioning, unlimited mileage, and mandatory liability insurance usually start between 40,000–60,000 esc. (US$200–300) per week. This figure does not include the 17% IVA tax or collision-damage waiver insurance. Fuel is costly: around 185 esc. per liter.

Entertainment. Nightclub and disco covers are high (2,000–4,000 esc.), as are drinks once inside (1,500 esc. and up). Concert tickets generally range from 1,000–7,000 esc.

Local transportation. Public transportation within the city — buses, trams, and the Metro — is very inexpensive, and taxis are affordable and a good way to get around (especially up all those hills). Most taxi rides within Lisbon's major neighborhoods will cost no more than 1,200 esc. Trains to the Estoril coast are very inexpensive (Sintra, 400 esc.).

Meals. Even top-rated restaurants may be surprisingly affordable compared to most European capitals. Portugal, like Spain, offers a mid-day meal bargain, the *ementa turística*, often costing no more than US$10–15 for a pre-fixe 3-course meal. Portuguese wines are quite good and very attractively priced (many between 2,000 and 4,000 esc./US$10–20), even in fine restaurants. A three-course dinner in a moderately priced restaurant (for one, with wine) should cost between 4,000–6,000 esc. (US$20–30). For an expensive meal in one of Lisbon's prestigious restaurants, expect to pay 8,000 esc. (US$40) and up, per person.

Museums. Admission fees range about 400–600 esc.; some days are free. Other sites and attractions may cost between 100–900 esc.

Sports. Golfing can be expensive in Lisbon: Greens fees go up to 20,000 esc. (US$100); horseback riding can go as high as 8,000 esc. (US$40).

CAMPING (*Campar*)
Portugal has a network of campsites, including several in the Lisbon area. Facilities range from basic to elaborate (swimming pools, tennis courts, bars and restaurants). **Camping Lisboa** (Parque Municipal de Campismo de Monsanto) has 400 individual camping bays and additional bungalows, swimming pool, tennis courts, and mini-golf. It's located in Monsanto Park, at Estrada de Circunvalação, 1500; Tel. 21-760 96 20; fax 21-760 96 33.

Lisbon

Information on camping can be obtained from tourist offices (see page 124), or the Federação Portuguesa de Campismo, Av. 5 de Outubro no. 15, 3°; Tel. 21-315 27 15, fax 21-54 93 72.

May we camp here?	**Podemos acampar aqui?**
We have a caravan (trailer).	**Nós temos uma roulotte.**

CAR RENTAL/HIRE (*Carros de Aluguer*)
(See also DRIVING on page 107)

If you wish to travel a good deal around the Lisbon area and see it at your leisure, renting a car is advisable. Major international firms, Avis, Hertz, Budget, National, and Europcar, are located both at the airport and in Lisbon; sometimes they have small satellite offices in other towns.

The minimum age for hiring a car is generally 21, and you must have a valid license held for at least one year. Rental companies will accept your home country's national driver's license. Third-party insurance is included in the basic charge but a collision damage waiver and personal accident policy may be added.

A sub-compact, four-door car with manual transmission, air conditioning, unlimited mileage, and mandatory liability insurance usually costs between 40,000–50,000 esc. per week. Costs may rise in high season (Easter and summer months). This figure does not include the 17% IVA tax. Pick-up and drop-off at different points is acceptable without surcharge, though doing either at the airport will incur a supplement of 3,300 esc.

For the lowest rates, arrange for a rental car in your home country. Ask for special seasonal rates and discounts, and find out what insurance is included. The IVA tax will have been included if you have pre-paid the car rental before arrival. Many credit cards automatically include full collision coverage if you use the card to pay for the car, but be sure to verify this before departure.

I'd like to hire a car today/ tomorrow.	**Queria alugar um carro para hoje/amanhã.**

| for one day/a week | **por um dia/uma semana** |
| Please include full insurance. | **Que inclua um seguro contra todos os riscos, por favor.** |

CLIMATE

Lisbon has an Atlantic climate influenced by the Mediterranean, which produces hot summers and mild winters. Spring and autumn are the best seasons to be in Lisbon, but in the summer, you can bask in the sunshine at the beaches west and south of the capital.

	J	F	M	A	M	J	J	A	S	O	N	D
Air temperature												
°C	12	12	14	15	18	21	23	24	22	18	15	13
°F	54	54	57	59	64	69	73	75	72	64	59	55
Sea temperature												
°C	15	16	17	18	19	21	21	20	19	18	16	14
°F	59	61	62	64	66	69	69	67	66	64	61	57

CLOTHING (*Roupa*)

Unless you come to Lisbon in an unseasonably cold winter, you'll never really have to dress warmly. Spring and autumn are relatively balmy, so you won't need anything heavier than a sweater in the daytime and light jacket at night. Summer days can be quite hot, but pack a wrap or sweater for cooler, windy evenings, and rainwear, just in case.

Lisboêtas dress fashionably but not formally. Virtually no establishments require a tie. The Estoril Casino "recommends" that men wear jackets in the evenings.

| Will I need a tie? | **É preciso gravata?** |
| Is it all right if I wear this? | **Vou bem assim?** |

CRIME AND SAFETY (See also POLICE on page 119)

Lisbon traditionally has been one of Europe's more laid-back and safe cities, but in recent years petty crime, especially targeting tourists, has become more common. Bag-snatching is increasing, so carry your handbag or camera bag firmly under your arm. Beware of pickpockets on buses, trams, and in cafés in the Rossio Square, the Alfama area, and other tourist spots.

In most parts of the Baixa and Bairro Alto, it is safe to walk at night. The occasionally seedy Rossio square and narrow, dark, and easy-to-get-lost-in streets of the Alfama district are best avoided at night; if you are going to a fado club in the latter, it's wise to take a taxi and have one called when you leave.

The beaches of the Estoril coast outside Lisbon are not reputed to be unsafe, but it is not a good idea to take any valuables, cameras, or purses to the beach.

As a general rule, keep valuables in the hotel safe and refrain from carrying large sums of money or wearing expensive jewelry. Report any theft to the hotel receptionist, the nearest police station, or the local tourist office. Leave nothing of value in parked cars, the easiest target for thieves; always lock cars and never leave cases, bags, cameras, etc., in view.

I want to report a theft.   **Quero participar um roubo.**

CUSTOMS AND ENTRY REQUIREMENTS (*Alfândega/Visto*)
American, British, Canadian, and many other nationalities need only a valid passport to visit Portugal. EU nationals may enter with an identity card. The length of stay authorized for most tourists is 90 days (60 for US and Canadian citizens).

Currency restrictions. Visitors from abroad can enter or exit Portugal with any amount of local or foreign currency, but sums exceeding the equivalent of 2,500,000 esc. in foreign currency must be declared on arrival.

Customs. Free exchange of non-duty-free goods for personal use is permitted between Portugal and other EU countries. However, duty-free items still are subject to restrictions: check before you go.

I've nothing to declare. **Não tenho nada a declarar.**

It's for my personal use. **É para uso pessoal.**

DRIVING (See also CAR RENTAL on page 104)

It is possible, but not advisable, to drive within Lisbon itself. Traffic is heavy and parking is extremely difficult. For most visitors, public transportation and private taxis are vastly superior methods of transport for navigating the city.

To bring your own car into Portugal, you will need your national driving license, registration papers and insurance — third-party coverage is obligatory — and the Green Card that makes your insurance valid in other countries.

Road conditions. In order of importance, Portugal's roads are as f ollows: *Auto-Estrada:* motorways (A1–A2, etc.); *Itinerário Principal*: highways (IP); *Itinerário Complementar*: Principal Route (IC); and *Estrada Nacional*: national roads (EN).

Rules and regulations. The rules of the road are the same as in most western European countries. Drive on the right. At roundabouts (traffic circles) the vehicle in the circle has priority unless road markings or lights indicate otherwise. Seat belts are compulsory in the front seats. Local driving standards are improving but are still erratic. In towns, pedestrians nominally have priority at crosswalks, but if you're walking, don't bank on it!

Speed limits are 120 kph (75 mph) on motorways, 90 kph (56 mph) on other roads, and 50 kph (37 mph) in urban areas. Minimum speeds are posted (in blue) for some motorway lanes and the suspension bridge across the River Tagus. Most motorways have tolls.

Fuel costs. Fuel prices are controlled by the government, and should be the same, or very close to it, everywhere you go. Many gas stations are 24-hour, and all accept credit cards. At presstime, the cost of fuel (*sem chumbo*) was 185 esc. per liter; diesel fuel (*gasoleo*) per liter cost 125 esc.

Parking. Unless there's an indication to the contrary, you can park for as long as you wish. Certain areas are metered. In "Blue Zones," you must buy a ticket from a machine for a designated time period; the ticket should then be displayed on the dash of the parked car. Car parks and garages are also available.

If you need help. If you belong to a motoring organization affiliated to the Automóvel Clube de Portugal (Rua Rosa Araújo 24; Tel. 21-356 39 31 or 21-942 50 95) you can use their emergency and repair services free of charge.

Road signs. Standard international pictograms are used in Portugal, but you might also encounter the following signs:

Alto	Halt
Cruzamento	Crossroads
Curva perigosa	Dangerous bend (curve)
Descida ingreme	Steep hill
Desvio	Diversion (detour)
Encruzilhada	Crossroads
Estacionamento permitido	Parking allowed
Estacionamento proíbido	No parking
Guiar com cuidado	Drive with care
Obras/Fim de obras	Road works (men working)/ end of road works
Paragem de autocarro	Bus stop

Pare	Stop
Passagem proíbida	No entry
Pedestres/peões	Pedestrians
Perigo	Danger
Posto de socorros	First-aid post
Proibida a entrada	No entry
Saída de camiões	Truck exit
Seguir pela direita/esquerda	Keep right/left
Sem saída	No through road
Sentido proíbido	No entry
Sentido único	One-way street
Silêncio	Silence zone
Stop	Stop
Trabalhos	Road works (men working)
Trânsito proíbido	No through traffic
Veículos pesados	Heavy vehicles
Velocidade máxima	Maximum speed
Are we on the right road for …?	**É esta a estrada para …?**
Fill the tank, please, super.	**Encha o depósito de super, por favor.**
Check the oil/tires/battery, please.	**Verifique o óleo/os pneus/ a bateria, se faz favor.**
I've broken down.	**O meu carro está avariado.**
There's been an accident.	**Houve um acidente.**

E

ELECTRICITY (*Corrente Eléctrica*)

Standard throughout Portugal is 220-volt, 50-cycle AC. For US appliances, 220v transformers and plug adaptors are needed.

I need an adaptor/a battery, please.	**Preciso de um adaptador/ uma pilha, por favor.**

EMBASSIES AND CONSULATES (*Consulado; Embaixada*)

Most embassies and consulates are open Monday–Friday from 9 or 10am until 5pm, with a break in the middle of the day of one or two hours.

Australia (use United Kingdom Embassy): Rua de São Bernardo 33; Tel. 21-392 40 00.

Canada (Embassy/Consulate): Avenida da Liberdade 144, 3°; Tel. 21-347 48 92.

Republic of Ireland (Embassy/Consulate): Rua da Imprensa à Estrela 1, 4°; Tel. 21-396 15 69.

South Africa (Embassy): Avenida Luís Bivar 10/10 A; Tel. 21-353 50 41.

United Kingdom (Embassy): Rua de São Bernardo 33; Tel. 21-392 44 00.

USA (Embassy/Consulate): Avenida das Forças Armadas 16; Tel. 21-727 33 00.

Where's the British/American embassy?	**Onde é a embaixada inglesa/ americana?**
It's very urgent.	**É muito urgente.**

EMERGENCIES (*Urgência*)

The following numbers are useful 24 hours a day in an emergency:

General emergency	**112**
Police	**21-346 61 41**
Ambulance (Red Cross)	**21-301 77 77**
Emergency road service	**21-942 91 03**

Although you can call the police from any one of the blue boxes in the street marked *polícia*, it's unlikely you'll get anyone on the other end who speaks anything but Portuguese.

G

GAY AND LESBIAN TRAVELERS
In a country heavily influenced by the Catholic Church, attitudes towards gays are not as tolerant as elsewhere in Europe. Lisbon is the most important city in Portugal's gay scene and offers a number of bars and clubs catering to a gay crowd, including Bar 106 (Rua de São Marcal 106); and Frágil (Rua da Atalaia 128). Also, on the Costa da Caparica, on the west coast of the peninsula across the Tagus, beach no. 9 on the narrow-gauge railway is gay. As yet, there are no help lines. A good web site with information in a number of languages is <www.portugalgay.pt>. It has information on travel, bars, beaches, and also has a message board.

GETTING THERE (See also AIRPORTS on page 101)
By Air. Lisbon's airport is linked by regularly scheduled daily non-stop flights from several European cities and from the East Coast of the United States. Flights from Canada, Australia, and New Zealand go through London or another European capital.

TAP/Air Portugal is the national airline: Tel. 888-328 26 71 from anywhere in Portugal; in Lisbon, 21-841 69 90; in New York, (212) 969-5775; in London, (171) 828-0262). From the US to Lisbon, TAP flies direct daily from New York and Newark, and once a week from Boston. Continental flies direct from Newark, and TWA from New

Lisbon

York. There are flights to the Portuguese capital aboard TAP and other carriers from all major European cities.

By Sea. Lisbon is, of course, a major port, and several cruise ships include a port-of-call in the capital, including Celebrity, Renaissance, Princess, Norwegian, and Royal Caribbean.

Ferries from Great Britain (Brittany Ferries) go to Santander, Spain, from Plymouth and Portsmouth, and to Bilbao, Spain from Portsmouth (P & O Ferries). Crossings take 24–36 hours. The drive from northern Spain to Lisbon is then likely to take another 12–14 hours.

By Rail. Portugal is linked to the European railway network; connections to Lisbon are possible from points throughout Spain, France, and the rest of continental Europe. Travel to Portugal is included on any EurailPass; the Eurodomino pass is available for travel within Portugal only, for a 3-, 5- or 10-day period, but may not be as good a deal as it is on more expensive rail networks in northern Europe.

The Portuguese national railway network is called **Caminhos de Ferro Portugueses** (Tel. 800 200 904, 21-888 40 25, or 21-811 20 00; <www.cp.pt>). The Santa Apolónia station (Avenida Dom Henrique; Tel. 21-888 40 25) serves all international trains.

Daily international trains run between Paris and Lisbon (Sud Express), crossing the frontier at Vilar Formoso; between Lisbon and Madrid, crossing the frontier at Marvão; and between Oporto and Vigo, crossing the frontier at Valença.

By Car. Major motorways connect other points in Europe to Spain and Portugal. The fastest route from Porto is the A1 *autoestrada*; from Madrid, take A2, crossing into the city at the Ponte 25 de Abril. The drive from Madrid to Lisbon is 8–10 hours; from Paris, 20–22 hours.

GUIDES AND TOURS (*Guias, Visitas Guiadas*)

All guides must belong to and meet the standards of the professional association of guides. A guide or interpreter can be hired directly through their association in Lisbon at Rua do Telhal 4, 3°; Tel. 21-346 71 70; open 9am–1pm, 2:30–6pm.

Information on half- or full-day city tours is available from the tourist information office (see page 124) or travel agents. **Transtejo** offers two-hour cruises on the River Tagus, showing off the city from the river, one of the only ways to take in the entire topography of the capital. They leave from Terreiro do Paço, April–October, daily at 11am and 3pm (Tel. 21-882 03 48; 3,000 esc.)

A **Belém Museum Tour** by mini-train (daily from 10am; 500 esc.) allows passengers to get on and off, and visits all the major museums in that monumental district, including Mosteiro dos Jerónimos, Museu da Marinha, Museu Nacional dos Coches, Museu Nacional de Arqueologia, Torre de Belém, Padrao dos Descobrimentos, and Centro Cultural de Belém. Call Tel. 21-393 19 85 for information and reservations.

All the excursion firms, such as **Portugal Tours** (Tel. 21-351 12 20), offer trips to Mafra, Queluz, Sintra, Cascais, and Estoril, as well as a long day's outing covering major sites north of Lisbon: Fátima, Alcobaça and Batalha, Óbidos, and Nazaré. If you are traveling independently, you can cover all these at greater leisure, even making an overnight stop or two on the way.

We'd like an English-speaking guide.	**Queremos um guia que fale inglês.**

H

HEALTH AND MEDICAL CARE

Standards of hygiene are generally very high; the most likely illness to befall travelers will be due to an excess of sun or alcohol. The water is safe to drink, but bottled water is available everywhere. Ask for *agua com gas* (carbonated) or *sem gas* (still).

Farmácias (chemists/drugstores) are open during normal business hours. At other times one shop in each neighborhood is on duty round the clock. Addresses are listed in newspapers. To locate night pharmacies, call Tel. 118.

For more serious illness or injury, the **British Hospital** (Rua Saraiva deCarvalho, 49; Tel. 21-395 5 67) has English-speaking staff.

Check your medical insurance to be sure it covers illness or accident while you are abroad. EU nationals with EU form E111, obtained before departure, can receive free emergency treatment at Social Security and Municipal hospitals in Portugal. Privately billed hospital visits are expensive.

Where's the nearest pharmacy?	**¿Aónde é a farmácia (de guardia) mais perto?**
I need a doctor/dentist.	**Preciso de um médico/dentista.**
Get a doctor quickly.	**Chame um médico, depressa.**
an ambulance	**uma ambulância**
hospital	**hospital**
an upset stomach	**mal de estômago**
sunstroke	**uma insolação**
a fever	**febre**

HOLIDAYS (*Feriado*)

1 January	*Ano Novo*	New Year's Day
25 April	*Dia da Liberdade*	Liberty Day
1 May	*Festa do Trabalho*	Labor Day
10 June	*Dia de Camões*	Camoens' Day
15 August	*Assunção*	Assumption
5 October	*Heróis da República*	Republic Day
1 November	*Todos-os-Santos*	All Saints' Day
1 December	*Dia da Independência*	Independence Day

| 8 December | *Imaculada Conceição* | Immaculate Conception |
| 25 December | *Natal* | Christmas Day |

Movable dates:

Carnaval	Shrove Tuesday/Carnival
Sexta-feira Santa	Good Friday
Corpo de Deus	Corpus Christi

Lisbon, Estoril, and Cascais have a local holiday on 13 June in honor of St. Anthony (Santo António). Sintra has a holiday on 29 June (São Pedro).

Are you open tomorrow?   **Estão abertos amanhã?**

LANGUAGE

Portuguese, a derivative of Latin, is spoken in such far-flung spots as Brazil, Angola, Mozambique, and Macau — all former colonies of Portugal. Your high-school Spanish may help with signs and menus, but will not unlock the mysteries of spoken Portuguese. The Portuguese spoken in Portugal is much more closed and gutteral-sounding, and is also spoken much faster than in Brazil.

Almost everyone understands Spanish and many speak French. A surprising number of people in Lisbon can speak a quite passable if not wholly fluent English. Schoolchildren are taught French and English.

The *Berlitz Portuguese Phrasebook and Dictionary* covers most situations you're likely to encounter during a visit to Portugal. Also useful is the *Berlitz Portuguese-English/English-Portuguese Pocket Dictionary,* containing a special menu-reader supplement.

See the front cover of this guide for a list of useful phrases. Here are some to get you going:

Lisbon

Do you speak English?	**Fala inglês?**
excuse me/you're welcome	**perdão/de nada**
please	**faz favor**
where/when/how	**onde/quando/como**
yesterday/today/tomorrow	**ontem/hoje/amanhã**
day/week/month/year	**dia/semana/mês/ano**
left/right	**esquerdo/direito**
near/far	**perto/longe**
cheap/expensive	**barato/caro**
hot/cold	**quente/frio**
old/new	**velho/novo**
Please write it down.	**Escreva-lo, por favor.**
What does this mean?	**Que quer dizer isto?**
Help me, please.	**Ajude-me, por favor.**
Just a minute.	**Um momento.**
What time is it?	**Que hora tem/é?**

Days:

Sunday	**domingo**
Monday	**segunda-feira**
Tuesday	**terça-feira**
Wednesday	**quarta-feira**
Thursday	**quinta-feira**
Friday	**sexta-feira**
Saturday	**sábado**
What day is it today?	**Que dia é hoje?**

M

MAPS (*Mapa*)
The tourist information offices in the capital have free maps of Lisbon and the surrounding area available, as well as a Carris map of the tram, bus, and elevator network. For most visitors these are sufficient, both for exploring Lisbon and reaching destinations beyond. Towns on the tourist circuit, such as Óbidos, Sintra, Cascais, and Estoril, also make free maps available through their local tourist information offices.

MEDIA (*Jornal, Revista, Rádio, Televisão*).
Europe's principal newspapers, including most British dailies and the *International Herald Tribune*, edited in Paris, are available on the day of publication at many newsagents and hotels. Popular foreign magazines are also sold at the same shops or stands. The most important Portuguese-language daily is *Diário de Notícias*, which contains full cultural listings.

Four television channels are widely available in Portugal: two are government-run and two are independent. Foreign films, whether made-for-TV or original cinematic productions, are usually shown in the original language with subtitles. Most hotels at the 4-star level and above have access to satellite reception that gets Sky, CNN, and others.

The government operates four radio channels. Program Two consists of classical music, while Program Four is mostly pop music. The Voice of America, BBC, Radio Canada International, and other foreign stations can be picked up on short wave.

Have you any English-language   **Tem jornais em inglês?**
newspapers?

MONEY (*Dinheiro*)
Currency (*moeda*). The national currency is the escudo, abbreviated esc. It is also officially abbreviated as PTE. Price tags at first look worrisome, since they usually involve many digits around a $ sign — which replaces the decimal point (5,000$00 esc means 5,000

escudos). The escudo is divided into 100 centavos, although you aren't likely to see centavo coins these days. Coins now in use are 1, 2, 5, 10, 20, 50, 100, and 200 esc. Banknotes come in denominations of 500, 1,000, 5,000, and 10,000 esc. At presstime, the exchange rate was: US $1 = 210 esc.; UK£1 = 317 esc.

The euro, the common European Union currency, was adopted in January 1999. Although prices appear in both escudos and euros, the euro remains an electronic banking currency until January 2002, when euro notes and coins will begin to circulate. After a transition period of six months, the escudo will be removed entirely from the market.

Currency Exchange (*banco, câmbio*). Normal banking hours are Monday–Friday 8:30am–3pm. In tourist areas, some banks remain open later and at weekends to change money, and there is a 24-hour exchange office at the airport. The exchange office at Santa Apolónia railway station is open 8:30am–8:30pm, and one bank in Praça dos Restauradores is open 6pm–11pm for the benefit of tourists.

Credit Cards (*cartão de crédito*). Standard international credit cards are widely accepted. In some shops and restaurants, especially in small towns outside Lisbon, however, you may not be able to use a credit card.

ATMs (*caixa automática*). Automatic teller machines outside banks, identified by the MB (MultiBanco) sign, are widely available. You can get cash (Portuguese escudos; maximum of 40,000 esc. per day) with a Visa or Mastercard or bank/debit card on one of the international networks like Cirrus or Plus, provided you have a personal identification number (PIN). The PIN number should be four digits.

Traveler's Checks. Less necessary now that ATMs have proliferated across the world, international traveler's checks can be cashed at any bank for a substantial flat fee; be sure to bring your passport.

Can I pay with this credit card?   **Posso pagar com cartão de crédito?**

I want to change some pounds/dollars.	**Queria trocar libras/dólares.**
Can you cash a traveler's cheque?	**Pode pagar um cheque de viagem?**

OPEN HOURS (*Horas de Abertura*)

Most shops and offices open 9am–1pm and 3–7pm weekdays, and Saturday 9am–1pm. Most museums are closed on Monday and public holidays (the tourist office has a full list of those open on Monday); palaces are closed on either Monday or Tuesday. On every other day (including Sunday) they are open 10/11am–5pm, but many close noon–2pm or 1–2:30pm. A number of shopping malls scattered around Lisbon and the suburbs are open 10am–10pm or even midnight, including Sunday.

open	**aberto**
closed	**fechado**
closed for repairs	**fechado para obras**
we're closed	**estamos encerrados**

POLICE (*Polícia*) (See also EMERGENCIES, page 110)

The national police, identified by their blue uniforms, are generally helpful and friendly and often speak a little English. Policemen assigned to traffic duty wear red armbands with a silver letter "T" (for Trânsito, or traffic) on a red background, a white helmet and white gloves. On highways, traffic is controlled by the Guarda Nacional Republicana (GNR) in white-and-red or white-and-blue cars, or on motorcycles. Occasionally they make spot-checks on documents or tires.

The emergency police telephone numbers are Tel. 21-346 61 41 (Public Security Police) and Tel. 21-347 56 38 (National Republican Guard).

Lisbon

Where's the nearest police station?	**Onde fica o posto de polícia mais próximo?**

POST OFFICES (*Correios*).

Lisbon's mail service is quite efficient. Mailboxes are of British pillar-box design and are painted bright red. Local post offices are open Monday–Friday 9am–6pm. Major branch offices also operate on Saturday until noon. A 24-hour office can be found at the airport. Lisbon's main post office in Praça dos Restauradores (opposite the tourist office) opens 8am–midnight daily. You can buy stamps from tobacconists and kiosks, and at post offices. A letter or postcard up to 20 g to EU countries costs 100 esc.; to the rest of the world, 140 esc.

Have you received any mail for …?	**Tem correio para …?**
A stamp for this letter/ postcard, please.	**Um selo para esta carta/este postal, por favor.**
express (special delivery)	**expresso**
airmail	**via aérea**
registered	**registado**

PUBLIC TRANSPORTATION (*Transporte*)

Local buses. Bus stops have signs indicating the numbers of buses that stop there, and many give details of their routes. You can get a free map of the entire transit system at tourist information offices, or at information posts of Carris, the local transport authority. Carris offices are at the base of the Santa Justa lift and Praça da Figueira. They also sell economical one- and four-day passes (*bilhete/passe turístico*), good on all buses and trams (but not the Metro). Call Tel. 21-361 30 00.

Most buses load from the front: You pay the driver or show him your pre-paid ticket before putting it in the clipping machine.

Trams. Tram stops are indicated by large signs marked *Paragem* (stop). The Carris bus map shows tram routes as well. Most trams are entered at the front, where you buy a ticket from the driver. On funiculars you pay at the door.

Metro. Lisbon's underground railway system, the Metropolitano, is clean, modern, and efficient, but it serves a limited area, mostly residential districts. The entry points are marked by an "M" sign. Charts of the system are displayed in every station and carriage. Directions in several languages are posted in the stations. Economical 10-trip tickets, 1- and 7-day tickets (*bilhete um dia, bilhete sete dias*) are available. Insert tickets in the small (and sometimes easy-to-overlook) electronic gates at the entrance.

Trains (*comboio*). Lisbon has four principal railway stations. International services and trains for northern Portugal leave from Santa Apolónia station, reached by bus 9 or 9A from Avenida da Liberdade. Commuter trains for the western suburbs and Estoril and Cascais leave from Cais do Sodré, while trains for Sintra and the west depart from Rossio station. The fourth station, called Sul e Sueste (South and Southeast), has ferryboats that cross the Tagus to connect with trains to the Algarve. The ticket price includes the ferry link. (See also Ferries below).

Taxis (*táxi*). Lisbon metered taxis, often Mercedes, are beige (although a few older ones are black with a green roof), indicated by a sign reading TAXI. In rural areas cars marked "A" (meaning *aluguer,* "for hire") operate as taxis, but without meters. Every neighborhood has a taxi stand, as do most railway, Metro, and ferry stations.

The fare is shown on the meter — check that it's running. Drivers add 20 percent after 10pm and extra if you have more than 30 kg (66 lb) of baggage. To request a taxi, call Tel. 21-815 50 61; Tel. 21-812 50 60; or Tel. 21-793 27 56.

Ferries. The two main ferry stations are next to each other: Sul e Sueste (the larger building, Praça do Comércio) and the Alfândega quay. The first serves only Seixal and Barreiro, from where south-bound trains depart (See "Trains" above). From the Alfândega quay, ferries run to

Lisbon

Cacilhas/Almada and Montijo. You can also catch the Cacilhas/Almada ferry at the Cais do Sodré ferry station near the railway station of the same name. From July to September, there are four ferry crossings a day between Sesimbra, Setúbal, and the peninsula of Tróia.

Inter-city buses. Lisbon's bus terminals serve different parts of the country. Ask about bus routes at the tourist office in Praça dos Restauradores. Buses are efficient and prices are reasonable.

How much is a ticket to …?	**Quanto é o bilhete para …?**
Will you tell me when to get off?	**Pode dizer-me quando devo descer?**
Where's the nearest bus/ tram stop?	**Onde fica a mais próxima paragem dos autocarros/ eléctricos?**
Where can I get a taxi?	**Onde posso encontrar um táxi?**
What's the fare to …?	**Quanto custa o percurso até …?**
bus	**autocarro**
car	**carro**
train	**trem**
tram (trolley car)	**eléctrico**
subway/underground train	**Metro**

R

RELIGION

The Portuguese are predominantly Roman Catholic, a fact reflected in surviving religious rituals and saints' days that are public holidays. The tourist information office has a list of services for English-speaking Catholics and other services.

The shrine at Fátima, recently visited by Pope John Paul II, is one of the most important pilgrimages in Catholicism.

T

TELEPHONE (*Telefone*)

Portugal's country code is 351. The local area code — 21 in the case of Lisbon and the Estoril Coast, including Sintra — must be dialed before all phone numbers, including local calls (9-digits total). Note that prefixes changed in October 1999, and you may still see old numbers in print. In such cases, a city code that begins with a "0" should be replaced by a "2" (i.e., "01" becomes "21"; "062" becomes "262").

White Portugal Telecom public telephones that accept both coins and prepaid telephone cards are found throughout the city. Coin boxes take 20, 50, and 100 esc coins; unused coins are returned. *Credifone* telephone cards can be purchased at post offices.

Local, national, and international calls made from hotels almost always carry an exorbitant surcharge. Use an international calling card if you must call from your hotel room. (Before departure, be sure to get the international access code in Portugal for your long-distance telephone carrier at home.)

To call, pick up the receiver, insert card or coin, wait for the dial tone, and dial the number. To make an international call, dial 00 for an international line (both Europe and overseas: UK 0044, USA 001) plus the country code plus the phone number (including the area code, without the initial '0' where there is one). If you wish to send a fax, you may do so from most hotels, though the charge may seem high.

collect call	**paga pelo destinatário**
Can you get me this number in …?	**Pode ligar-me para este número em …?**

Lisbon

TIME ZONES *(Hora Local)*

In 1992 Portugal switched time zones to align with most of the European Union. Now it is at GMT + 1 in winter, making sunrise rather late. From the last Sunday in March until the last Sunday in October, the clocks are moved one hour ahead for summer time, GMT + 2. In summer the chart looks like this:

New York	London	Paris	**Lisbon**	Sydney	Auckland
6am	11am	noon	**noon**	8pm	10pm

TIPPING *(Serviço, Gorjeta)*

Hotel and restaurant bills are generally all-inclusive, but an additional tip of 5–10 percent is common and even expected in restaurants. Hotel porters, per bag, generally receive 100 esc. Give hairdressers and taxi drivers 10 percent, tour guides 10–15 percent. Lavatory attendants should get about 50 esc. and your hotel room cleaner about 100 esc. per day.

TOILETS *(Lavabo, Quarto de Banho, Serviços)*

Public toilets exist in some large towns; however, almost every bar and restaurant has one available for public use. While it's polite to buy a coffee or drink if you drop in to use the restroom, no one will yell at you for not doing so.

Restrooms are marked *Senhoras* (ladies) and *Homens* (men).

Where are the toilets? **¿Onde é o lavabo/quarto de banho?**

TOURIST INFORMATION *(Informação Turística)*

Portuguese National Tourist Offices (ICEP, or Investimentos, Comércio e Turismo de Portugal) are maintained in many countries:

Canada: Suite 1005, 60 Bloor Street West, Toronto, Ont. M4W 3B8; Tel. (416) 921 7376.

Ireland: 54 Dawson Street, Dublin. Tel. 353-670 9133.

South Africa: 4th floor, Sunnyside Ridge, Sunnyside Drive, PO Box 2473 Houghton, Johannesburg. Tel. (2711) 484 3487.

United Kingdom: 22/25 Sackville St, London W1X 1DE; Tel. (071) 494 1441.

USA: 590 Fifth Ave, 4th floor, New York, NY 10036; Tel. (212) 354 4403.

In Lisbon, the main tourist information office is in Palácio Foz, on Praça dos Restauradores; Tel. 21-346 36 43. There is also an office at the airport (Arrivals Terminal).

A recently inaugurated **help line** for tourist information, the *linha verde turista,* is Tel. 0800-296 296. The free service, in Portuguese, English, French, and Spanish, is available Monday–Saturday 9am–midnight, and Sunday and holidays 9am–8pm. Information on sights, hotels, restaurants, transportation, hospitals, and police is available.

Where is the tourist office?   **¿Onde é o turismo?**

W

WEB SITES AND INTERNET CAFÉS *(Cafés Cibernéticos)*
Here are some web sites worth checking out before you go: <www.portugalvirtual.pt> (general country information and tourism database, with accommodations links); <www.portugal.org> (the official web site of the Portuguese tourism office); <www.tap.pt> (site of Tap/Air Portugal, the Portuguese national airline); <www.cp.pt> (site of Caminhos de Ferro Portugueses, the national railway network, with timetables and information on international and domestic trains); <www.pousadas.pt> (site of government-owned pousadas).

The tourist information office has a full list of internet *(ciber)* cafés in Lisbon — at least 11 at last count — where travelers can go to check e-mail for a reasonable hourly (or partial-hour) fee. Two convenient places are Ciber-Chiado (Largo do Picadeiro, 10; Tel. 21-346 67 22; 600 esc/per hour), and Espaço Agora (Rua da Cintura do Porto de Lxa, Armazém 1/Naves 3, 4 and 5; Tel. 21-394 01 70; 300 esc./per hour)

WEIGHTS AND MEASURES
The metric system is used in Portugal.

Lisbon

Length

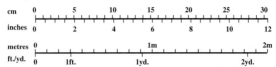

| cm | 0 | | 5 | | 10 | | 15 | | 20 | | 25 | | 30 |
| inches | 0 | | 2 | | 4 | | 6 | | 8 | | 10 | | 12 |

| metres | 0 | | 1m | | 2m |
| ft./yd. | 0 | 1ft. | 1yd. | | 2yd. |

Weight

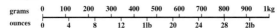

| grams | 0 | 100 | 200 | 300 | 400 | 500 | 600 | 700 | 800 | 900 | 1kg |
| ounces | 0 | 4 | 8 | 12 | 1lb | 20 | 24 | 28 | 2lb | | |

Temperature

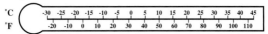

| °C | -30 -25 -20 -15 -10 -5 0 5 10 15 20 25 30 35 40 45 |
| °F | -20 -10 0 10 20 30 40 50 60 70 80 90 100 110 |

Fluid measures

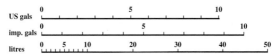

US gals	0	5	10
imp. gals	0	5	10
litres	0 5 10	20	30	40	50

Distance

| km | 0 | 1 | 2 | 3 | 4 | 5 | 6 | 8 | 10 | 12 | 14 | 16 |
| miles | 0 | ½ | 1 | 1½ | 2 | 3 | 4 | 5 | 6 | 7 | 8 | 9 | 10 |

Y

YOUTH HOSTELS (*Pousadas de Juventude*)

Contact the Associação Portuguesa de Pousadas de Juventude at Avenida Duque de Ávila 137, 1000 Lisbon; Tel. 21-355 90 81. There are two youth hostels in the immediate Lisbon area. Pousada de Juventude de Lisboa (Rua Andrade Corvo, 46; Tel.21-353 26 96, fax 21-353 75 41; Metro: Estação de Picoas) is the larger, with 146 beds. Pousada de Juventude (Via de Moscavide, L 47-101 Parque das Nações; Tel. 21-892 08 90, fax 21-892 08 91) has 72 beds.

Recommended Hotels

Hotel prices in Lisbon have risen in recent years to match most western European destinations, even surpassing popular cities like Barcelona at the top levels. Many hotels offer special packages (such as summer or weekend reductions).

Central Lisbon covers the area from the waterfront, Bairro Alto, Lapa, and Avenida da Liberdade. North Lisbon refers to the area around and beyond Praça Marquês de Pombal. Pousadas, found beyond Lisbon, are government-owned hotels and inns; the ones listed occupy historic buildings, and their restaurants are usually among the town's best.

The price indication given is for a double room, with breakfast, including service and taxes (currently 5 percent of room price) in high season (generally April–October).

$$$$$	over 40,000 esc
$$$$	30,000–40,000 esc
$$$	20,000–30,000 esc
$$	12,000–20,000 esc
$	below 12,000 esc

CENTRAL LISBON

As Janelas Verdes $$$–$$$$ *Rua das Janelas Verdes, 47; Tel. 21-396 81 43; fax 21-396 81 44;* <www.heritage.pt>. A charming and elegant hotel in the sophisticated Lapa district, near the River Tagus and Museu de Arte Antiga. This small hotel occupies the 18th-century townhouse of one of Portugal's most famous writers, Eço de Queirós, and has recently expanded into the home next door. Has a quiet, garden-like courtyard and top-floor library, and some rooms have superb views of the river. Wheelchair access. 29 rooms. Major credit cards.

Hotel Britania $$$ *Rua Rodrigues Sampaio, 17; Tel; 21-315 50 16; fax 21-315 50 21;* <www.heritage.pt>. Owned by the same family that runs two other top, intimate hotels in Lisbon, the Britania, in a historic 1940s townhouse, may be the most comfortable of them all. The rooms are spacious and elegantly appointed, with marble bathrooms. The hotel, near Av. Liberdade in the center, has been lovingly restored and boasts lovely Art Deco and clubby touches, such as the bar. Wheelchair access. 30 rooms. Major credit cards.

Hotel Apartamento Orion Eden $$ *Praça dos Restauradores, 24; Tel; 21-321 66 00; fax 21-321 66 66; e-mail <eden.lisboa@ mail.telepac.pt>*. In a famous Art Deco building right on Praça dos Restauradores, this modern apartment-hotel is a great deal, especially for families. There are kitchen-equipped studios and full apartments, with daily or weekly maid service. Panoramic pool and breakfast service. Wheelchair access. 134 rooms. Major credit cards.

Hotel Avenida Palace $$$$ *Rua 1 de Dezembro, 123; Tel. 21-346 01 51; fax 21-342 28 84; <www.hotel-avenida-palace.pt>*. Right on Rossio, the major plaza in the Baixa district, the recently remodeled Avenida Palace is one of Lisbon's finest luxury hotels. It has a magnificent Old World feel, with sumptuous public rooms and elegant, classically decorated accommodations. Sybarites can opt for the Louis XVI-style room. Wheelchair access. 82 rooms. Major credit cards.

Lapa Palace $$$$$ *Rua Pau da Bandeira, 4; Tel. 21-395 00 05; fax 395 06 65; <www.orient-expresshotels.com>*. This lovingly detailed conversion of a palatial old mansion overlooks the River Tagus in Lapa. Opened in 1992, it remains the trendsetter in Lisbon luxury. Grounds are covered in landscaped gardens, and there is an outdoor pool. Rooms are plush, with azulejo-decorated bathrooms; the entrance, swathed in marble and ceiling frescoes, is enough to make you swoon. Wheelchair access. 102 rooms. Major credit cards.

Recommended Hotels

Hotel Metropole $$$ *Rua 1 de Dezembro, 123; Tel. 21-346 01 51; fax 21-342 28 84; e-mail <almeida_hotels@ip.pt>.* One of Lisbon's best deals, this classic Art Deco 1920s hotel is in the heart of the Baixa, overlooking Rossio square. Rooms are generously sized and outfitted with period antiques. Wheelchair access. 36 rooms. Major credit cards.

Hotel Tivoli Lisboa $$$$ *Avenida da Liberdade 185; Tel. 21-319 89 00; fax 21-319 89 50; e-mail <htlisboa@mail. telepac.pt>.* One of Lisbon's largest and longest-running luxury hotels, right on the main thoroughfare, Av. Liberdade. The Tivoli excels in services and facilities, which include a noted rooftop restaurant, a heated outdoor swimming pool, and tennis courts, a true rarity in the city. Outdoor dining in summer. Wheelchair access. 327 rooms. Major credit cards.

Lisboa Plaza $$$ *Travessa do Salitre 7 (off Av. Liberdade); Tel. 21-346 39 22; fax 21-347 16 30; <www.heritage.pt>.* This stylish and recently renovated family-run hotel, on a quiet street off Avenida da Liberdade, opened in the 1950s. Rooms are exceedingly comfortable and every detail has been carefully overseen by a noted Portuguese designer. A restaurant serves the usual Portuguese specialties and a generous buffet breakfast. Wheelchair access. 116 rooms. Major credit cards.

Lisboa Regency Chiado $$$ *Rua Nova do Almada, 114; Tel. 21-325 61 00; fax 21-325 61 61; e-mail <regencychiado@ madeiraregency.pt>.* Lisbon's newest hotel, opened in early 2000, is this chic number occupying part of the rebuilt Armazéns do Chiado shopping mall, in the heart of the Chiado district. In keeping with the upscale surroundings, the lobby and rooms are very design-oriented. It's likely to become very popular soon; for now, it's a bargain. Wheelchair access. 40 rooms. Major credit cards.

Lisbon

Veneza $$$ *Avenida da Liberdade, 189; Tel. 21-352 26 18; fax 21-352 67 00.* A charming small and historic hotel right on the main drag of Lisbon. This former Venetian-style, 19th-century palace has a spectacular spiral staircase and period touches, like stained glass windows, throughout. In 10 years it has drawn a strong following. Wheelchair access. 37 rooms. Major credit cards.

York House $$$$ *Rua das Janelas Verdes 32; Tel. 21-396 27 85; fax 21-397 27 93; e-mail <yorkhouse@mail.telepac.pt>.* Near the Museum of Ancient Art, in Lapa, several blocks west of the center, this converted 17th-century convent overlooks the River Tagus. The hotel retains the feel of a serene retreat from the outside world. Rooms are elegant but not stuffy. Outdoor dining in the garden courtyard during the summer and a recommended on-premises restaurant. Wheelchair access. 34 rooms. Major credit cards.

NORTH LISBON

Dom Pedro Lisboa $$$$$ *Av. Eng. Duarte Pacheco, 24; Tel. 21-389 66 00; fax 21-38966 01.* Lisbon's newest 5-star hotel, and perhaps the city's swankest entry, is this mirrored high-rise, just north of Parque Edward VII and across from the Amoreiras shopping mall. Rooms, equipped with every luxury, have spectacular views of the city. Dom Pedro has supplanted more traditional luxury hotels in Lisbon in just three years. Popular with American tourists and European business travelers. Top-flight Italian restaurant. Wheelchair access. 263 rooms. Major credit cards.

Four Seasons Hotel The Ritz $$$$$ *Rua Rodrigo da Fonseca, 88; Tel. 21-383 20 20; fax 21-383 17 83; <www.fourseasons.com>.* One of Lisbon's oldest luxury hotels certainly has pedigree in its names. Its ugly Soviet-style exterior could not be a greater contrast to its swank interior, which was recently remodeled and is the height of indulgence. Rooms with balconies with good views over Parque Eduardo VII and busy Pombal square. Excellent restaurant, Veranda. Wheelchair access. 284 rooms. Major credit cards.

Residencia Astória $ *Rua Braancamp, 10; Tel. 21-386 13 17; fax 21-386 04 91.* The handsome exterior may outclass the rooms, but this mid-size 1920s-style hotel in an elite part of town, just off Praça Marquês de Pombal, ranks as a bargain. Popular with both backpackers and older travelers looking for a deal. Rooms are plain but comfortable. 30 rooms. Major credit cards.

GRAÇA

Albergaria Senhora do Monte $$ *Calçada do Monte, 39; Tel. 21-886 60 02; fax 21-887 77 83.* Perched on a hillside in Graç, a district northeast of Baixa, this simple-looking place offers good-value accommodation with considerable charm and excellent views of St. George's Castle and the river. Has a garden courtyard, where guests can take their breakfasts. 28 rooms. Major credit cards.

ESTORIL COAST

Hotel Albatroz $$$$–$$$$$ *Rua Frederico Arouca 100, Cascais; Tel. 21-484 73 80 and 21-483 28 21; fax 21-484 48 27;* <www.albatrozhotel.pt>. Cascais's most elegant hotel is this mansion perched above the Praia da Rainha beach. Public rooms and accommodations swim in luxury. In May 2000, the Albatroz expanded into another beautiful palace across the street. Outdoor pool and nice restaurant with superb views. 46 rooms. Major credit cards.

Hotel do Guincho $$$$ *Guincho Beach, Tel. 21-487 04 91; fax 21-487 04 31.* Just outside of Cascais, in a former 16th-century fortress perched on a rocky ledge overlooking Guincho beach and the sea, this boutique hotel is a remarkable getaway. Marvelous antique touches throughout, including tile floors and period silver and crystal. Most rooms have fireplaces, and many have balconies with views of the sea — including Cabo da Roca, Europe's westernmost point. 36 rooms. Major credit cards.

Hotel Estoril Sol $$$$$ *Avenida Marginal, Cascais; Tel. 21-483 90 00; fax 21-483 22 80; <www.hotelestorilsol.pt>.* Towering high over the bay of Cascais, with great views, this huge, older-style luxury resort hotel has freshwater and seawater pools, squash courts, health club, and sauna. Wheelchair access. 317 rooms. Major credit cards.

Hotel Palácio do Estoril $$$ *Rua do Parque, Estoril; Tel. 21-468 04 00; fax 21-468 48 67.* This luxury hotel, established in 1930, looks like a cruise ship and is as palatial as its name suggests. Has undergone a major renovation. Heated outdoor pool, tennis, and gardens. Special rates for guests at its golf course. Top-notch restaurant, Four Seasons. Wheelchair access. 162 rooms. Major credit cards.

QUELUZ AND SINTRA

Palacio de Seteais $$$$–$$$$$ *Rua Barbosa do Bocage, 8, Sintra; Tel. 21-923 32 00; fax 21-923 42 77; e-mail <hpseteais@mail.telepac.pt>.* A luxury hotel in a beautiful and historic 18th-century palace with antique furniture, manicured gardens, and superb views. Some visitors find it a bit dainty compared to more relaxed *quintas* nearby. Lord Byron wrote in the gardens here. Sports facilities include tennis courts and outdoor pool. Horseback riding. 30 rooms. Major credit cards.

Pousada de D. Maria I $$–$$$$ *Largo do Palácio, Queluz; Tel. 21-435 61 58; fax 21-435 61 89; <www.pousadas.pt>.* Occupying the part of the royal summer palace that was the domain of the Royal Guard of the Court, this pink pousada, which only opened in 1995, is ideal if you want to explore Lisbon and its surroundings but aren't really keen on staying in the city. Accommodations are attractive and a good size, and Cozinha Velha, the restaurant that's part of the palace across the road and is now associated with the government-owned pousada, is one of the area's best. 26 rooms. Major credit cards.

Quinta da Capela $$$ *Estrada Velha de Colares, Sintra; Tel. 21-929 01 70; fax 21-929 34 25.* A beautiful, rambling 16th-century house on an old country estate, 3 km (2 miles) outside Sintra. Seven handsome, understated rooms in the main house, and three private cottages with self-catering. The gorgeous grounds, shared with swans and peacocks, are ideal for a relaxed retreat. The chapel is still used for Mass on Sunday. No restaurant. Closed November–March (cottages open year-round). 11 rooms. Major credit cards.

Quinta das Sequóias $$$ *Estrada de Monserrate, Sintra; Tel/fax 21-9243 38 21; fax 21-923 03 42.* A comforting and welcoming 19th-century manor house surrounded by beautiful grounds full of redwood trees, perfect for long walks. Rooms are large and handsomely outfitted with period furniture. Swimming pool and Jacuzzi. Closed December–January. 6 rooms. Major credit cards.

SOUTH OF LISBON

Quinta das Torres $$$ *Estrada Nacional 10, Vila Fresca de Azeitão; Tel. 21-218 00 11; fax 21-219 06 07.* A 16th-century mansion with lived-in charm, 15 km (9 miles) outside of Setúbal amid peaceful, relaxing grounds. The delightful rooms have ceramic tiles, religious art, and antiques. Two suites have private terraces and fireplaces, and there are two private bungalows, with kitchens, that sleep four. 12 rooms. Major credit cards.

Pousada de Palmela $$$ *Castelo de Palmela, Palmela; Tel. 21-235 12 26; fax 21-233 04 40;* <www.pousadas.pt>. A luxury pousada carved out of a 12th-century hilltop castle looking toward Setúbal and the sea. Notable restaurant serving local dishes, especially seafood. 28 rooms. Major credit cards.

Pousada de São Filipe $$$ *Castelo de São Filipe, 2900 Setúbal; Tel. 265-52 38 44; fax 265/53 25 38;* <www.pousadas.pt>. A luxury pousada inside the walls of a fortress built in 1590, overlooking the port of Setúbul. Great views of the Sado estuary and Tróia peninsula. Some rooms in the former castle's dungeons. Close to the Serra de Arrábida National Park. 14 rooms. Major credit cards.

NORTH OF LISBON

Estalagem do Convento $$ *Rua João d'Ornelas, Óbidos; Tel. 262-95 92 17; fax 262/95 91 59.* A handsome and inviting former nunnery right outside the town's ancient walls. The comfortable rooms have period antiques. A commendable restaurant with a pretty patio. 31 rooms. Major credit cards.

Pousada do Castelo $$$$ *Paço Real, Óbidos; Tel. 262-95 91 05; fax 262/95 91 48;* <www.pousadas.pt>. The pousada in greatest demand in Portugal, it was the first to be fashioned from a historic monument. This tiny inn is lodged in the medieval castle inside the walled town. Three suites occupy the battlement towers. Stunning views of the whitewashed village and surrounding countryside. Reserve well in advance. 9 rooms. Major credit cards.

Quinta do Campo $$ *Valado dos Frades, Nazaré; Tel. 262-57 71 35; fax 262/57 75 55.* Family-run accommodation is in a charming old manor house, once part of an old monastic estate, just 5 km (3 miles) from Nazaré on the road to Alcobaça. Swimming pool, tennis and beautiful gardens. Dinner is available if prior notice is given. 8 rooms. Major credit cards.

Recommended Restaurants

The Lisbon dining scene has gotten much more diverse in recent years. The Bairro Alto is still one of the best areas for eating out, since it's densest with restaurants of all stripes; but, as Lisbon moves to embrace the river again, restaurants have been popping up along the old dock areas — Doca de Alcântara, Doca do Poço do Bispo, and Doca Jardim do Tabaco — and along the riverfront near the Parque das Nações, where Expo 98 was held.

Even the top restaurants in Lisbon are fairly affordable by the standards of European capitals. The "tourist menu" (*ementa turística*) in many restaurants, especially at lunchtime, can be an excellent value at 1,500–2,500 esc, with either wine, beer, mineral water, or a soft drink included.

The prices indicated are for starter, main course, and dessert, with wine, per person. (Note that some fish or shellfish dishes will be more expensive.) Service and IVA of 16 percent are included, as they generally are in the bill. All restaurants listed here accept major credit cards.

Many Lisbon restaurants close for the entire month of August.

$$$$	over 8,000 esc
$$$	5,000–8,000 esc
$$	3,000–5,000 esc
$	below 3,000 esc

BAIRRO ALTO

Cervejeria da Trindade $–$$ *Rua Nova da Trindade 20; Tel. 21-346 08 08.* Open daily for lunch and dinner (until late). A famous old beer hall and restaurant, in a former monastery decorated with azulejo-covered walls. Extremely popular Portuguese cooking and seafood specialties at good prices.

Lisbon

Casa Nostra $$-$$$ *Travessa do Poço da Cidade, 60;* Open Tuesday–Friday, Sunday for lunch and dinner; Saturday, dinner only. A good-looking dining room in a converted old house, "Our House" features an authentic Italian menu with excellent carpaccios, vegetables, and pastas.

Conventual $$ *Praça das Flores 45; Tel. 21-390 91 96.* Open Monday–Friday for lunch and dinner; Saturday, dinner only. Closed August. A former convent just west of the busy Bairro Alto, this reserved restaurant is one of Lisbon's best, serving fine Portuguese cuisine.

Mesón El Gordo $$-$$$ *Rua de Sao Boaventura, 16; Tel. 21-342 42 66.* Open Thursday–Tuesday dinner, until late. A Spanish-inspired tavern with a ceiling painted like the sky, hams hanging over the bar, boisterous late-night diners munching on tapas, and a variety of Portuguese, Spanish, and French dishes.

Pap d'Açorda $$-$$$ *Rua da Atalaia 5–597; Tel. 21-346 48 11.* Open Tuesday–Saturday for lunch and dinner; Monday, dinner only. One of Lisbon's hippest spots, cool but disarmingly informal and popular with a wide-ranging clientele, including the local cultural elite. Traditional and creative Portuguese dishes with fabulous and filling *açorda real* (a thick shellfish stew with lobster and shrimp) as the main specialty. Attentive service.

Securas $-$$ *Calçada do Duque, 27; Tel. 21-342 85 14.* Open daily for lunch and dinner. A simple little restaurant perched on a stairway with million-dollar views of Alfama and St. George's Castle across the way. Straightforward Portuguese fare made special if you secure a table outdoors on the stairs.

Tavares $$$-$$$$ *Rua da Misericórdia 37; Tel. 21-342 11 12.* Open Monday–Friday for lunch and dinner; Sunday, dinner only. A stylish and immensely popular restaurant-café with ornate ceilings, mirrors, and chandeliers. Serving classical French cuisine for more than a century.

CENTRAL LISBON

Bico do Sapato $$$ *Avenida Infante D. Henrique (Cais da Pedra); Tel. 21-881 03 20.* Open daily for lunch and dinner. One of Lisbon's newest and most chic restaurants, this former warehouse on the waterfront across from Santa Apolónia station is trendy, but rightly so. The funky decor is cool but not overdone. Excellent and fairly priced creative Portuguese menu and a good list of local wines.

Bonjardim $ *Travessa de Santo Antão, 10; Tel. 21-342 74 24.* Open daily for lunch and dinner. More mess hall than restaurant, this large and gregarious place is terrific for low-key, filling, and dirt-cheap Portuguese cooking. The roasted chicken with crisp fries seems to be the signature dish. Annex across the street.

Martinho da Arcada $$$ *Arcadas do Terreiro do Paço/Praça do Comércio; Tel. 21-886 62 13.* Open Monday– Saturday for lunch and dinner. Lisbon's oldest café, under the arcades at Praça do Comércio, dates back to 1778 and has a colorful history littered with political and literary figures, frequented by the likes of Fernando Pessoa. Today it is a national monument and still a great, atmospheric place for a bite to eat.

A Confraria $$$ *Rua das Janelas Verdes (in York House hotel); Tel. 21-36 24 35.* Open daily for lunch and dinner. Inhabiting the former 17th-century convent of the refined and retreat-like York House, this is a cut above a typical hotel restaurant. Eugénia Cerqueira creates a daily menu with imaginative interpretations of

Portuguese cuisine. The classic-looking restaurant spills out onto a beautiful, quiet courtyard. Excellent desserts.

Casa da Comida $$$$ *Travessa das Amoreiras 1; Tel. 21-388 53 76.* Open Monday–Friday for lunch and dinner, Saturday dinner only. Closed August. An elegant but not stuffy, handsomely decorated restaurant in northwest Lisbon near the aqueduct. Fine Portuguese and French cuisine served outdoors in a patio setting in an old mansion. A good place to blow the bank roll.

Gambrinus $$$$ *Rua das Portas de Santo Antão 25; Tel. 21-342 14 66.* Open daily for lunch and dinner (until late). A sophisticated and elegant restaurant, one of the city's finest and most famous, near Rossio. Specializes in traditional Portuguese and Galician dishes, which means fresh seafood.

Tágide $$$$ *Largo da Academia Nacional de Belas Artes 18; Tel. 21-342 07 20.* Open Sunday–Friday for lunch and dinner. This classic Portuguese and French restaurant is situated west of the Praça do Comércio in an elegant, old house offering magnificent views of the waterfront, cathedral and square. Popular with the expense-account crowd.

A Travessa $$$ *Travessa das Inglesinhas, 28; Tel. 21-390 20 34.* Open Monday–Friday for lunch and dinner, Saturday dinner only. A Belgian- and French-influenced menu with dishes such as mussels, stuffed eggplant, and bacon-wrapped dates enlivens this good-looking place near Parliament. Look for an A Travessa to open near the river on Terreiro do Paço.

Alcântara Café $$$$ *Rua Maria Luísa Holstein, 15; Tel. 21-362 12 26.* Open daily for dinner. One of the restaurants of the moment, this handsome place, equal parts industrial and post-modern, is the goal of many of Lisbon's socialites on any given night. The menu is unique, but receives some mixed reports. Still, customers get what they come for — buzz.

Café-Café $$$ *Rua de Cascais, 57; Tel. 21-361 03 10.* Open Monday–Saturday for dinner. Giving Alcântara Café a run for its money as a beacon for beautiful people, Café-Café draws crowds with its sleek modernist design and Portuguese nouvelle cuisine. The bar is on the first floor, the restaurant on the second, where tables surround a grand piano. Major credit cards.

THE DOCKS

Doca de Santo Amaro $$$–$$$$ *Alcântara Mar.* Most places here open daily for lunch and dinner. Lisbon began renovating warehouses along the river docks to re-embrace the Tejo. Doca de Santo Amaro, near the 25 de Abril bridge, is the best-known of the city's docks and has a lively bar-and-restaurant scene. The best idea here is to stroll along the dock and choose a restaurant that looks appealing and vibrant. Some to look for include: **Café In** (Av. Brasilia, 311); **Doca 6** (Armazem, 6); and **Espalha Brasas** (Armazen, 12).

Doca do Poço do Bispo $$–$$$ *Cais do Sodré.* With Lisbon's hosting of Expo 98, the city has moved to reincorporate the riverfront area east of downtown. Many new restaurants, bars, and clubs have moved in. Several are concentrated around Rua da Cintura do Porto de Lisboa, near Avenida 24 de Julho, including **Rock City** (Cais do Santos); **Docks** (Armazem H, 226); and **Indochina** (Armazem H, 230).

Doca do Bom Sucesso. **$$$–$$$$** *Belém.* This small marina in Belém has become a popular nightlife spot for business people and politicos. Restaurants are predictably upscale and fashionable, including **Vela Latina** and **Spazio Evasione**.

Doca Jardim do Tabaco *Avenida Infante D. Henrique, Pavilhão A–B; tel. 21-882 42 80.* Just east of Praça do Comércio, between Casa dos Bicos and Santa Apolónia train station is a series of popular docks now converted into restaurants. They look out over the Tejo River as well as the historic Alfama district. Restaurants include **Pinchos, Jardim do Marisco, Figaro,** and **Rodizio.**

O Nobre $$$$ *Edifício Nau, Marina Expo 98; Tel.21-893 16 04.* Open Monday–Saturday for lunch and dinner. Long one of Lisbon's top restaurants, O Nobre recently installed in the Marina of the Parque das Nações (Expo 98). It doesn't appear to have lost a step, continuing in its tradition of providing exquisite, classic Portuguese cooking. Service is very professional and attentive.

ALFAMA

Casa do Leão $$ *Castelo de São Jorge; Tel. 21-87 59 62.* Open daily for lunch only. The only restaurant located just inside the castle ramparts and serving a wide range of traditional international and Portuguese dishes. Excellent views.

BÉLEM

São Jerónimo $$ *Rua dos Jerónimos, 12; Tel. 21-364 87 96.* Open Monday–Friday for lunch and dinner, Saturday for dinner only. A sleek, beautifully designed restaurant with warm woods, attractive dimmed lighting, and leather chairs, just around the corner from the *Jerónimos monastery.* The menu is creative Portuguese.

O Caseiro $ *Rua de Belém 35; Tel. 21-363 88 03.* Open Monday–Saturday for lunch and dinner. Closed August. In a convenient location between the Coach Museum and the monastery, this is an informal but intimate restaurant serving simple but tasty local dishes. Specialties include *porco á alentejana* (pork, Alentejo style).

NORTH LISBON

Ristorante Il Gattopardo $$$ *Av Eng. Duarte Pacheco, 24 (in Hotel Dom Pedro); Tel. 21-389 66 22.* Open daily for lunch and dinner. Major credit cards. Ensconced on the third floor of the swank new Dom Pedro Hotel, this thoroughly Italian restaurant shouldn't be overlooked just because it's in a hotel. It serves excellent pastas, as well as meat and fish dishes.

António Clara $$$–$$$$ *Avenida da República 38; Tel.21-796 63 80.* Open Monday–Saturday for lunch and dinner. Closed last two weeks in August. For formal, refined dining, this restaurant, well known for its exquisite French and international cooking, is considered one of the best in Lisbon. Magnificently housed in a stylish Art Nouveau palace.

OUTSIDE LISBON

Cozinha Velha $$$ *Palácio Nacional de Queluz, Largo do Palácio, Queluz; Tel. 21- 435 02 32.* Open daily for lunch and dinner. One of the most atmospheric restaurants in Portugal, this was once the old kitchen of the royal palace. It has a garden patio and a decor that will transport you to the 17th century. The regional cooking is excellent.

Colares Velho $$–$$$ *Largo Dr. Carlos França, 1–4, Colares (Sintra); Tel. 21-929 24 06.* Open daily for lunch and dinner. A small and charming restaurant in the village of Colares, a few miles down the mountain road from Sintra, owned by the people who run Quinta da Capela. The dining room is like the library of a country estate. Dishes are imaginative and professionally done. Homemade desserts and good daily specials.

INDEX